MODERN HISTORIOGRAPHY

MODERN HISTORIOGRAPHY

An Introduction

Michael Bentley

London and New York

First published 1999 by Routledge
11 New Fetter Lane, London EC4P 4EE

Simultaneously published in the USA and Canada
by Routledge
29 West 35th Street, New York, NY 10001

© 1999 Michael Bentley

Typeset in Ehrhardt by Keystroke, Jacaranda Lodge, Wolverhampton
Printed and bound in Great Britain by Clays Ltd, St Ives plc

All rights reserved. No part of this book may be reprinted or reproduced
or utilized in any form or by any electronic, mechanical, or other means,
now known or hereafter invented, including photocopying and recording,
or in any information storage or retrieval system, without permission in
writing from the publishers.

British Library Cataloguing in Publication Data
A catalogue record for this book is available from the British Library

Library of Congress Cataloging-in-Publication Data
Bentley, Michael
Modern historiography : an introduction / Michael Bentley.
p.   cm.
Includes bibliographical references.
1. Historiography. I. Title.
D13.B427   1999
907'.2–dc21   98-39603
CIP

ISBN 0–415–20267–1

CONTENTS

CONTENTS

PREFACE

Most of this brief account first appeared in 1997 as part of a large-scale study of historiography, edited by the present writer and published by Routledge under the title *Companion to Historiography*. There were and are strong arguments for leaving it there. The piece had taken shape in an attempt to provide some context for a number of essays aimed at analysing recent currents in historical thinking; and to that extent the self-conscious positioning of trends and schools and moods that the reader will find in this essay defies easy translation into a free-standing survey. It too readily acquires an authorial voice that descants without ground bass or counterpoint such as the sister studies offered in the *Companion*. Not only that, but the accompaniment of many pieces that had explored the nature of historiography before the onset of the modern era (or had done so in an Asian or Middle-Eastern setting) made it possible to throw those using the *Companion* into the Enlightenment or romantic period with only a cursory allusion to what had gone before and without any serious comparative ambition. The text assumes, in other words, that the reader is already well down the runway with engines roaring: those still taxi-ing may feel with some justification that they deserve a smoother departure and wish to return to the gentler pace of the larger study.

Perhaps these and other considerations made it necessary that any recommendation to excerpt the piece should come from someone else.

The suggestion came initially from an old friend and colleague, R. I. Moore, who asked Routledge to look into the possibility of reissuing the essay as a short book. Following some discussion and helpful reports from readers, we decided to go ahead with this proposal, largely on the strength of two considerations. First, the larger volume had been intended for reference collections in libraries and its cost placed this brief account beyond the pocket of most students and faculty. There seemed much sense in finding a format that would allow an inexpensive paperback issue of the most 'immediate' section of it so that students could use it in studying their history courses or as part of a general approach to the subject. But a second thought also appeared germane. Something approaching a revolution in the status and content of historiography is currently underway; and it struck both author and publisher that some good might be done by making this review of recent discussion more widely available at once.

Time was when 'historiography' featured as an optional extra in university and college curricula. Students would be made to sit an examination in 'General History' (deemed the more challenging for its never having been taught); or possibly some aged member of staff would cast his or her thoughts across a lifetime's empirical work in the archives and tell an audience what history was about. Or large classes of students, especially in the US, would find themselves in a 101-style survey of 'classic' historical writing which could find a fit with World Civs as a staple of undergraduate education. None of these approaches deserves to be despised: some of them were well-judged and effectively presented. Occasionally a student would be fired by experiencing them into taking a genuine interest in historical assumptions and tendencies or into thinking more critically about a particular author or text. What united this sort of teaching, all the same, was a sense of luxury, of icing on the cake. It might be made 'interesting', but until around 1970 few teachers raised the awkwardness that historiography ought to be seen as a crucial ingredient in the cake itself rather than its superficial decoration. Now, undoubtedly, the running together of 'history' and 'historiography' into an intellectual form in which one eliminates and substitutes for the other has become pernicious: it makes no more sense to argue for fusion than it does for treating one of the elements as redundant. And in recent years a rather trite form of postmodern 'understanding' – triter for the unbearable vacuities of its vocabulary –

has implied that history is finished as a form of intellectual enquiry because it has been shown to reveal nothing but what historians happen to believe at any particular period – a conclusion which 'historiography' is supposed to prove. None the less we live in a world whose 'turn' towards postmodern questions has done inestimable good in shaking one of the more conservative disciplines to its foundations and giving rise to much innovative and intelligent writing. Rarely has a generation had the opportunity of the current cohort of students to rethink what history means. Very heaven is it now to be young, bright and eager to think about the past and what the study of it can yield. This is the environment in which historiography has moved to centre-stage as a core element in any historical education, and this is the rationale for reflections such as the ones offered in this sketch of historiographical developments since the Enlightenment.

'Historiography' means at least two things and this account is about only one of them. At its highest level of originality, an historiographical statement may attempt an enquiry which former generations would have been happier to call 'philosophy of history' in an applied form. It might range from Hegel's bewildering and magical visions of time's patterns, through Marx's extraordinary penetration of them, on towards Dilthey's never-written *Critique of Historical Reason* to the works of Croce and Ortega y Gasset and Raymond Aron in Europe, of Oakeshott and Collingwood in Britain. At a less elevated, but no less original level, modern analytical historiography has produced instances of deep-structural enquiry which has brought to the surface important aspects of a particular writer or school of historical writing. Such work has left virtually no major historian of the nineteenth or early-twentieth centuries looking now as he or she looked twenty years ago. Researchers have taken their own questions – moulded inevitably by the intellectual climate that has fastened itself on the West over the last quarter-century – and used them to expose layers of meaning and possible connections with worlds outside history that had eluded scholars who had brought no less intelligence and training to their texts but whose objectives and starting-points had sent them elsewhere. So when we now review the historical work of Edward Gibbon or Thomas Carlyle or Jules Michelet or Theodor Mommsen or the nineteenth-century's historical titan, Leopold von Ranke, the shelves contain critical accounts which locate these authors in ways that would not have been attempted until quite recently. The task of supplying such critiques, which often seem as demanding to read as to write, falls to the historiographer and one definition of historiography is that it is the class or set of all such studies.

But that is not what this book does. How could it in so short an account of so many historians? What we shall be examining in these pages is rather a subject that once might have been labelled 'the history of historiography'. The task lies not in providing an original reading or interpretation of any single writer or school but instead to seek freshness of viewpoint by offering a synthetic account which searches for connection and comparison and which is not afraid to look beyond the subject of history for explanation of what historians do and how they think. It seeks sophistication less in its depth than in its width and in the shaping of its narrative – one of many that could have been contrived – to explain developments with maximum clarity. Nor does a history of this kind escape its contemporary climate any more than would a substantive history of the period or a detailed analysis of a given writer. Just as the modern historiographer applies an older 'philosophy of history' in new ways, so an historian of historiography moves beyond what a previous generation might have believed to be relevant or appropriate; and the result is a text that has a different scope and an expanded sense of what historical 'knowledge' might be taken to include. The greatest historiographer of the twentieth century, Arnaldo Momigliano, knew more about historical writing than the present writer could ever pretend to know; and his work will live on undimmed into the next century. Yet even he supplies a fascinating case in point, since his own horizons of explanation were formed during the turbulent politics and positivist intellectual environment of the 1930s and 1940s. When he constructed his insights into the working of an historical mind, he made them from within that horizon and asked the questions that seemed most urgent within the mental landscape around him. In the longer perspective we have of his work and from inside a different *Weltanschauung*, the commentator has himself become an object of study, the historiographer an example of his own subject. No one will 'supersede' Momigliano; but we may choose to see his world through lenses he did not have and paint in colours he would have avoided.

'Are you a postmodernist?' The tedious question emerges pretty quickly among gatherings of historians nervous of historiography and terrified by 'theory'. It is meant to carry the same force that 'Are you a Protestant?' might have exerted during the Counter-Reformation. It is a bad question in that it has no serious or unambiguous answer. Those who reply in the negative are often historians whose work suggests that they are in fact irremediably steeped in the poison they pride themselves on having refused to swallow. Equally, those who adopt the label with triumphal complacency are often underpowered individuals who would welcome any *argot* that made them appear discerning intellectuals. Better, perhaps, to move beyond an assumed contrast of position and recognize, quite simply, that the form and content of discussion throughout the humanities since the 1970s have shifted in ways that have produced distinctive approaches to many of the concepts that historians assume every day – knowledge, under-standing, imagination, explanation, analysis, narrative – and that, whether the result has been desirable or not, no one but a hermit in a cave is likely to have remained unaffected by some of them if only in self-conscious reaction. Indeed consciousness itself has been the victor in this dubious *jihad*. We may not all be postmodernists but we are, each of us, more self-conscious about what we are trying to achieve in writing history (and about the obstacles in our way) than the generations of the 1950s, say, had any reason to be. Complaints heard everywhere that history has become obscure rest on an important truth as well as a weary groan. Historians have lost some of their transparency because they have learned that historiography teaches blurredness in its constant assertion of cultural interference and the predominance of standpoint. Once allow historiography a role in an understanding of how history fashions itself, therefore, and complexity comes in through every pore with its contested assumptions and tortured *mentalités*.

Horizons of explanation and landscapes of the mind form part of the texture of this introductory volume. To those who accuse it of super-ficiality I submit immediately. Many specialist writers know more about all the historians mentioned here than the present writer and all of them know more about one or two. I have ransacked the writing of others in order to compose my account and gladly acknowledge the help and expertise of those without whom no general view could be achieved. Sometimes, however, specialists spend more time looking down than across; and very knowledgeable scholars, let alone students, can learn a little by glancing sideways to see how history was *constructed* in a different country or former epoch. 'The past is a foreign country' has become historiography's most persistent *cliché* as well as its most worthless. For the very description that the past can never fulfil is that of a visitable place or space: its essential no-where-ness and no-thing-ness is what makes us project our images of it. This little book is about those images as they are implied in historical accounts written at various moments and in a number of intellectual locations over the past two hundred years. Not unreasonably in an introduction, it does no more than introduce. If one student picks it up and comes away thinking that history is a good subject because it makes the mind turn by challenging it to explain why the past looks the way it does, and why it once looked some other way, then the project will attain its objective. If one professional historian glances at it and finds three sentences that stimulate a cultural comparison or a tremor in perspective, then it will more than serve its modest purpose.

PRELUDE

'Modernity' carries a number of resonances and dangers as we review developments in historical thought and practice over two of its most critical centuries. Not least, it invites a collapse into precisely one of those developments – the nineteenth-century notion of a 'Whig' understanding of history – which would see the period as a process of constant 'advances' towards a sophisticated present from a primitive past, giving prizes along the way to those historians who sound precocious and patronizing those who do not. But it seems important to establish some base-lines to the enquiry and to give necessary shape to an account which, reduced to a list of great writers and random subjects, would become as long and boggling as the period itself. It was in this period that history discovered its identity as a discipline: a distinctive way of organizing and representing knowledge. During these years its practitioners acquired the rationale, the techniques and the self-awareness that would lead to their displaying the characteristics that we think of as 'modern' attributes in historiography. They exhibited source-criticism at new forensic levels; they created texts of massive proportion and complex structure; they deployed ideas picked up from other kinds of enquiry; they talked and argued and quarrelled about how the job should be done in a vocabulary quite unavailable to Suetonius or Bede, Guiccardini or Bodin. The story cannot be read, however, as a single narrative. It is better seen as a series of overlapping

1

(and often contradictory) moods and doctrines whose interaction we must heed and explain if the account is to go beyond a roll of honour or the flat description of forgotten books.

Standing back from any specific works of history, one can ask immediate questions about the character of eighteenth-century historiography before its character underwent a series of shifts in the intellectual revolution known as the Enlightenment. It was the product, plainly, of a distinctive environment which had felt the effects of an epoch of scientific advance in the generation of Sir Isaac Newton (1642–1727). This new climate supplied a fresh sense of time itself, wrenching temporal understanding away from the relativistic models that had seemed natural to medieval authors and substituting a notion of absolute time that passed independently of the world whose changes it measured – a notion deeply embedded in all views of the past until the twentieth century offered a fundamental revision in the wake of a second revolution in science and philosophy.[1] More tangibly, the offensive mounted by science and the astringent philosophies of Descartes, Spinoza and Locke could not but exert pressure on divine explanations of the universe and, by extension, on its past. These ideas, plus the reverberations of a changing order in the growth of states and their mutual relationships, helped give rise to what Eric Voegelin called a dominant 'sense of epoch' in the new century:

> We do not find before 1700 a comprehensive interpretation of man in society and history that could take into account the constituent factors of the new situation, that is: the breakdown of the Church as the universal institution of Christian mankind, the plurality of sovereign states as ultimate political units, the discovery of the New World and the more intimate acquaintance with Asiatic civilizations, the idea of the non-Christian nature of man as the foundation for speculation on law and ethics, the demonism of the parochial, national communities and the idea of the passions as motivating forces of man. Only after 1700 does the cumulative effect of these various factors make itself felt in the acute consciousness that, in the aggregate, an epoch has come to an end and that the new situation requires a gigantic effort of interpretation in order to recover for the existence of man in society and history a meaning which could substitute for the lost meaning of Christian existence.[2]

---

1 I simplify here part of the thrust of an interesting argument about modern conceptions of time: see Wilcox 1987. Cf. Whitrow 1988; Rotenstreich 1987.
2 Voegelin 1975: 5. For more details see Maner 1982.

This view has implications. It means that Bossuet's *Universal History* of 1681 had lost much of its contemporary relevance before the book reached its audience.[3] It means that one needs to be cautious before declaring eighteenth-century writing 'empirical', as modern writers often do,[4] partly because empiricism (in so far as it involves a lack of theoretical assumption) is impossible in practice and unthinkable in the abstract, partly because these authors responded to a series of stimuli which made their work look devoid of concepts since they were attempting to defy overarching explanations of the world familiar to their grandfathers. Certainly those who seriously addressed the status of knowledge as an issue began with the questions raised by 'empirical' science; but the thought applies little to those writing history who had their own priorities and starting-points. Dr Johnson's kicking against a stone in order to refute a philosophical enemy was more sophisticated (because more pointed), after all, than its violence suggests; and historians, in kicking against their own forms of contemporary resistance, did not operate randomly or in innocence. So robust a thinker as Dr Johnson understood, for example, the distinction between 'a journal, which has regard only to time, and a history which ranges facts according to their dependence on each other, and postpones or anticipates according to the convenience of narration'.[5] His contemporaries also used the language of 'anachronism' as a form of criticism: there are examples of it in English from the mid-seventeenth century. Two terms escaped currency, however, until around 1780: the idea of a 'period' of history designating a stretch of time with an internal unity;[6] and, more important, the notion of a

---

3 Bossuet (1681) had been neither universal nor informed by the critical techniques of the French school associated with Jean Mabillon whose *De Re Diplomatica* was published in the same year. It perpetuated divine motivation as the guiding force in the world. A recent study is Meyer 1993.

4 e.g. Patrick Gardiner (1959: 5), who believes that 'a strong emphasis upon considerations of an empirical character remains its most striking feature'; cf. Haddock 1980: 73; Jann 1985: xvi–xix.

5 Samuel Johnson to Mr Cave, n.d. (*c*.1742), in James Boswell, *The Life of Samuel Johnson LL.D.* (2 vols, 1791), I, 155. By a 'journal' Johnson obviously has in mind what later historical thinkers refer to as 'chronicle'.

6 I do not mean to overlook earlier deployments of 'period' in the more limited sense of conveniently divided units of time such as 'ages' or 'centuries': we see those

'source' understood as comprising one of the elements out of which a historical text might flow just as a river originates in its source. William Robertson in his history of America seems to have been the first to use the word in that sense in 1777.[7] What was absent in historical thinking for the first three-quarters of the eighteenth century seems, from a modern perspective, quite as suggestive as what was present.

Another characteristic of that thinking makes one think hard again about the allegation of empiricism. For one of the most prevalent modes of representing the past lay in creating moral lessons with historical events as their illustrations. The view that history was fit only for 'philosophy teaching by example' did not originate in the eighteenth century: it occurs in classical writers and Renaissance writers rediscovered it (Culler 1985: 4). But Lord Bolingbroke's *Letters on the Study and Use of History* (1752) gave the concept a contemporary cachet and few authors of his day avoided giving a patina to their text that was intended to elevate the mind of the reader or bend it towards a particular conclusion. This operation was not carried out empirically; it required authors to come to their task with a sense of commitment, even if they would have had difficulty in defining the message that they intended to convey.

The early eighteenth century had sometimes gone beyond such expressions of doctrine, especially in Italy where it had done so at two levels. So far as historical practice went, the monumental work of collection and edition associated with Ludovico Muratori (1672–1750) – 'the grandfather of modern historiography'[8] – brought a distinguished tradition of Italian writing since the Renaissance to a conclusion in the twenty-eight volumes of *Rerum Italicarum Scriptores*, which began to appear in 1723 and was remarkable for its precocity seen against instances of the nationalistic search for origins that characterizes

---

in various forms from the Renaissance onwards. For coverage of this wider period, see Hay 1977.

7 Robertson 1777. Robertson (1721–93), was Principal of Edinburgh University and Historiographer Royal. The study of America followed two volumes on the *History of Scotland* (1759) and three volumes on the reign of Charles V.

8 Hay 1977. Muratori was aware of the work of the Maurists and went on to prepare a vast collection of documents intended to throw light on the medieval period in Italy, the *Antiquitates Italicae Medii Aevi* (1738–42). He also wrote about theatre, ethics and religion.

so much European historiography in the first half of the nineteenth century. At a second level of argument, however, Italian precocity ran still deeper. In his own lifetime Giambattista Vico (1668–1744) remained all but unknown, a struggling and impoverished professor of rhetoric at the University of Naples. When he died his ideas died with him. Only when the French historian Jules Michelet rediscovered and popularized his thinking did Vico's originality as an historical thinker begin to emerge. In the twentieth century, with its absorption in the nature of language and its relationship to what holders of a given vocabulary can think and what they cannot, he has become almost a guru, particularly since Vico meets most modern norms of intellectuality by having lived a thankless life marked by incessant adversity. His *New Science* (1725–44) is now often read as the first serious treatment of the issues raised in modern philosophy of history, marking the moment when historical thinking came of age.

We can say at once that much of this recent opinion verges on the absurd. In the first place, other scholars could match the range of ideas that we associate with Vico, none more powerfully than another Neapolitan historian, Pietro Giannone (1676–1748), who wrote a successful history of the kingdom of Naples.[9] Vico's own historical writing, dating from the early part of his life, remained completely traditional.[10] His Catholicism not only endured (unlike Giannone's) but formed an element in rationalizing his views about history, chopping off significant areas of human enquiry as raising questions answerable only by God. Chief among these was the natural world – since God made it, only he could comprehend it – but Vico held that man made something, too: he constructed, through the various epochs of his history, the civil society in which he lives. Because he had made it, moreover, he could, in principle, discover the truth about it. This idea, Vico's *verum factum* principle, formed the starting-point for much of his thought about why history mattered and why the vaunted new 'science' of the Newtonians would remain

---

9 I am grateful for John Robertson's correction over this point. A prescient series of remarks about the strength of Giannone appears in Barnes 1962: 129–30.

10 *De antiquissima Italorum sapientia ex linguae Latinae originibus eruenda* (3 vols, Naples, 1710). But there had been a hint of things to come in his dissertation on methodology, *De nostri temporis studiorum ratione* (1708).

chimerical. Certainly the world needed a new science but it would not find one in mathematics or physics but rather by focusing on what man, with his restricted faculties, might competently investigate. This task, he sees at once, raises problems of its own and, since no one has addressed them,

> we must proceed as if there were no books in the world.
>
> But in this dense night of darkness which enshrouds earliest antiquity so distant from us, appears the eternal light, which never sets, of this truth which is beyond any possible doubt: that the civil world has itself been made by men, and that its principles therefore can, because they must, be rediscovered within the modifications of our own human mind. And this must give anyone who reflects upon its cause to marvel how the philosophers have all earnestly endeavoured to attain knowledge of the natural world which, since he made it, God alone knows, and have neglected to meditate upon this world of nations, or civil world, knowledge of which, since men had made it, they could attain.

(Vico 1982: 198)

It was an arresting proposition but would remain no more than that unless Vico could suggest a better method of research than meditation.

This he did and hinted at its content in the word 'modifications'. Now some nineteenth-century writers (and particularly Vico's countryman, Benedetto Croce) fastened on the term in order to make Vico sound as though he had been born a follower of Hegel a century too soon (cf. Walsh 1976: 144). In fact, Vico had groped his way towards an idea of the greatest importance. He believed that societies changed non-randomly, that each phase of their changing needed to be seen as part of an entire series and that at each point in their development they exhibited characteristics – and only those characteristics – that were appropriate to their location in this process of transformation. As Isaiah Berlin expressed it,

> in the individual and society alike, phase follows phase not haphazardly (as the Epicureans thought) nor in a series of mechanical causes or effects (as the Stoics taught) but as stages in the pursuit of an intelligible purpose – man's effort to understand himself and his world, and to realise his capacities in it.

(Berlin 1976: 34–5)

The modifications in world-view that Vico writes about have to be seen in this light: they give a clue to the moments when history moves from one phase to another. And the clue to the modifications comes, as one might expect from a professor of rhetoric, in language. So long, therefore, as we can reconstruct the vocabulary of past civilizations, we can re-enter their thought world and understand their history.

What Vico said about the past, as opposed to how to study it, was far less impressive. In Book Four of the *Scienza Nuova*, he invents a series of rigid triads, 'the three sects of times which the nations profess in the course of the lives' (Vico 1982: 250). Rather 'the' than 'their' because the course is common: it takes the form of an endless cycle of advance and regression – *corsi e ricorsi* – as all societies proceed from an age of gods, through an age of heroes to an age of men; and then back to the beginning again. Each age produces distinctive configurations, so one has three kinds of nature, three of custom, three of natural law, three of civil statehood, and so on. None of this seems plausible but it hardly matters. What Marx and others were to take away from Vico was a sense of how historical change might be viewed and investigated. In the long term his ideas would help form one vital pole of argument about history that affected discussion until the First World War.[11] In the short term he was, like the rest of us, dead. His death in 1744 left the intellectual world untroubled, the content of historical writing unchanged and its centre of gravity not in Naples but in Paris.

---

11 His life and work have come under recent revaluation in Lilla 1993.

1

THE ENLIGHTENMENT

Many of the characteristics attributed promiscuously to eighteenth-century historiography become more persuasive when directed at a special form of it: that inspired by the renaissance (primarily French) of ideas and cultural ambitions which modernity has come to call the 'Enlightenment'. This intellectual environment (at its most intense between, say, 1750 and 1790) gave rise to historical enquiry of a marked character and one by no means shared by other countries in other decades. It promoted a singular sense of the present as a moment of exceptional importance and weight in the history of the world. The *philosophes* of Paris seemed transparently pleased to be living in the eighteenth century and to have transcended the Greek and Roman cultures by which their contemporaries elsewhere still appeared obsessed. 'European elites had lived since the Renaissance with a culture borrowed from antiquity,' writes François Furet,

> a period whose artists and authors represented unsurpassable models and whose literary genres constituted the authoritative canons of beauty and truth. Now Europe was raising the question of its cultural autonomy: the academic quarrel between 'ancients' and 'moderns' in France at the end of Louis XIV's reign ultimately centred on the notion that classical culture was not a past but a present.
>
> (Furet 1984: 81)

Because the present had won a new pedigree at the expense of the past, only parts of the past interested the Enlightenment. Its prophets retained a veneration for the classical world; and they displayed a new enthusiasm for quite recent history which would show how their own superior culture evolved. In theory such a sense of evolution might produce a conception of the long-term transitions from ancient to modern times, as one of the Enlightenment's most suggestive exemplars, Condorcet, implies in the introduction to his best-known historical essay:

> All peoples whose history is recorded fall somewhere between our present degree of civilisation and that which we still see among savage tribes; if we survey in a single sweep the universal history of peoples we see them sometimes making fresh progress, sometimes plunging back into ignorance, sometimes surviving somewhere between these extremes or halted at a certain point, sometimes disappearing from the earth under the conqueror's heel, mixing with the victors or living on in slavery, or sometimes receiving knowledge from some enlightened people in order to transmit it in their turn to other nations, and so welding an uninterrupted chain between the beginning of historical time and the century in which we live.
>
> (Condorcet 1795: 8)

But pieties of this kind rarely transcended theory. In practice the Enlightenment amused itself with celebrated figures in modern history such as Charles XII or Louis XIV. One much-recalled text, Voltaire's *Essai sur les mœurs* of 1756, did, it is true, attempt a more ambitious survey of world history in order to frame an answer to Bossuet's despised work of 1681, though even there the novelty appeared more in the territory covered geographically than in the periods Voltaire treated chronologically. For the most part, however, the Enlightenment omitted from its purview periods of history that it found distasteful and, since the whole of the Middle Ages was found coarse and untutored, this meant that medieval history had little presence in Paris.

Enlightened history discovered grounds for satisfaction in the present and to this extent it harboured philosophical pretensions. Indeed, one notices at once that its spokesmen – for they are mostly men – established reputations as philosophers, mathematicians, statesmen or *belle-lettristes* before taking to history. Once having taken to it, they displayed an undercurrent of opinion about the past which might be reduced to three central properties. First, they argued a position that shrieked secularism. The easiest prediction to make about any work inspired by the French Enlightenment is that it will attack organized religion and betray that sardonic anticlericalism found in most other statements by the *philosophes*. Second, they reflected a cynicism about the motivations and moral capacities of individuals while elevating *l'esprit humain* to new levels of moral authority, thus granting the impersonal force what they denied in its agents. Third and most significant, they constructed texts in which satire does not stop at the clerics but rather forms a crucial part of the tone for the entire enterprise. The story turns out well because it turns out in the present; and the telling of the story can therefore afford a certain buoyancy. Wit consequently does service for thought but often does it brilliantly. The result is the opposite of tragedy. Each author brings to the task a different collection of skills and moods, but the general point requiring stress is one made by Hayden White: that the Enlightenment bequeathes no tragic history just as (and for the same reason that) it leaves no tragic literature. Its satire functions not as a decorative motif in its texts but as a fundamental mode of representation (White 1973: 66).

If there seems less satire than elsewhere in Condorcet's posthumous *Esquisse* of 1795, then the circumstances of its writing more than explain the peculiarity. He had enjoyed a life in which talent and noble birth coalesced to make him secretary of the Académie des Sciences by the time he was 30. The Revolution proved his undoing. He had collaborated in it at first but opposed the new Jacobin constitution and found himself forced into hiding. After his detection and arrest he was thrown into prison where he died in 1794, possibly by his own hand. His essay reflecting on the history of humanity stems from these last, difficult years; and although the tone lacks the cockiness of Voltaire, the text offers perhaps the most rounded illustration of Enlightenment method and assumptions in their application to history. Montesquieu (1749) had been more profound in his better-known comparative study of law but Condorcet presents a more relevant model to those wishing to form a view of the French Enlightenment's tendencies in historiography.

Like Vico, Condorcet thinks in threes. Humanity's history falls into three stages. The first runs from the darkness of an unknowable primitivism up to the development of language; our views of it rest necessarily on conjecture and travellers' tales. A second phase, hardly more accessible to the present, moves from the coming of language to the introduction of alphabetic writing which Condorcet invests with signal importance. The third phase comprises, simply, everything else. Because he sees the second stage as having been completed by the time of the Greeks, this latter section of history runs from the classical period to the present. From this point forward in the narrative the historian does have access to the truth via the writings of contemporaries and the epoch offers a continuum,

> linked by an uninterrupted chain of facts and observations. . . . Philosophy has nothing more to guess, no more hypothetical surmises to make; it is enough to assemble and order the facts and to show the useful truths that can be derived from their connections and from their totality.

> (Condorcet 1795: 9)

He then goes on to subdivide his three phases into a further triad of which the last is the most interesting. It begins with the revival of science and the development of printing; it proceeds to show how science later threw off the yoke of 'authority'; and that leaves the author with the present – a culture about which he can feel optimistic, despite his own misfortunes, because science will point the way to the future. His first book had been a study of integral calculus. In a real sense his last one was, too.

Perhaps the absorption with philosophy and science militated against the production of a great French historian in this generation. The French had to wait until the Revolution became the focus of modern experience and the stuff of a new history that Michelet would make his own fifty years later. The country which ought to have produced an enlightened historiography – America, the child of Parisian ideas – again did not do so in a significant form before 1800. Instead the extension of 'enlightened' thought into historical practice occurred elsewhere, most notably in Scotland and England.

That Scotland should have received the teaching of France will surprise no one familiar with the traditional affinity between the two societies. It is especially well reflected in the biography of David Hume (1712–76) whose *History of England* (1754–62) constitutes a *locus classicus* for those exploring the Enlightenment's sense of history. Still known to the British Library Catalogue as 'David Hume *the Historian*', he is better known (and with good reason) as a philosopher. Hume had spent many years alternating between Europe and Britain before accepting a post in 1752 as librarian to the Faculty of Advocates in Edinburgh where he had access to the sources that would allow him to write history. He intended from the start that his historical books would make some money to compensate for the abysmal sales of his philosophical works. And since the more recent periods of the English past attracted both him and his likely audience, and 'being frightened with the notion of continuing a narrative through a period of seventeen hundred years' (Hume 1754–62: I, xi), he began there and wrote the story backwards, in effect, over the next decade. The 'first' volume on the Stuarts caused him constant grief because of allegations that followed relating to its sympathy with Charles I and the Stuart cause; and those insinuations (that he was a Tory historian blind to the virtues of the Whig revolution of 1688) certainly diverted attention from the degree to which Hume reflected the presuppositions of the Enlightenment throughout the work.

Not that his philosophical sophistication interfered with the text: one of its surprises lies in the degree to which Hume forgot his own doctrines, over causation for example, the moment he turned to writing about past events. Indeed, he forgot about so much that it becomes tempting to see neither an enlightened nor an unenlightened historian in Hume so much as a bad one *tout court*. But the echoes of Parisian salons occur too frequently for that. He shared the loathing of Paris for barbarous epochs such as the Anglo-Saxon period and dismissed them as quickly as possible without any need for research:

> We can say little, but that they were in general a rude, uncultivated people, ignorant of letters, unskilled in the mechanical arts, untamed to submission under law and government, addicted to intemperance, riot and disorder. . . . The conquest put the people in a situation of receiving slowly from abroad the rudiments of science and cultivation, and of correcting their rough and licentious manners.
>
> (ibid. I, 305–6)

Even in the Stuart volume, Hume's Parisian assumptions shine through the narrative, despite his fondness for romance in the pre-Civil War years, in his treatment of evidence and readiness to use the conjectural method when speaking of matters for which he has no evidence at all. Consider what he cannot possibly 'know', for example, in one of his most famous passages – that describing the execution of Charles I in 1649:

It is impossible to describe the grief, indignation, and astonishment, which took place, not only among the spectators, who were overwhelmed with a flood of sorrow, but throughout the whole nation, as soon as the report of this fatal execution was conveyed to them. . . . On weaker minds, the effect of these complicated passions was prodigious. Women are said to have cast forth the untimely fruit of their womb: others fell into convulsions, or sank into such a melancholy as attended them to their grave: nay, some, unmindful of themselves, as though they could not, or would not, survive their beloved prince, it is reported, suddenly fell down dead. The very pulpits were bedewed with unsuborned tears.[12]

These methods are less grossly exposed in William Robertson of Edinburgh, whose histories of Scotland and America, beside his better-known study of Charles V, suggest a wider vision and a more historical mind.[13]

England's relations with the Continent notoriously had a different tone from the Scottish, but Edward Gibbon's travels had long since overcome any sense of distance. The death of his father in 1770 led him to settle in London; he had lived before then mainly in Lausanne and had travelled considerably. The famous visit to Rome had occurred in 1764 and intention became reality from 1768 when he began the narrative of *The Decline and Fall of the Roman Empire* (1776–88), which by the end of the nineteenth century attained the status of Boswell on Johnson as a work of literature and which today remains the one historical study that most educated people would identify as an example of eighteenth-century historical writing. That he had a grasp greater than either Boswell or Johnson of the issues raised by a large-scale historical project had apparently eluded both of them in a three-way conversation of 1775 to which Boswell gives us an allusion:

JOHNSON. 'We must consider how very little history there is; I mean real authentick history. That certain Kings reigned, and certain battles were fought, we can depend upon as true; but all the colouring, all the philosophy of history is conjecture.'

---

12 Ibid. VIII, 137–8. For the significance of the 'conjectural' approach, see Peardon 1933; 10–11 and *passim*.

13 Robertson's books enjoyed a long life as well as extraordinary sales by eighteenth-century standards. Edward Freeman later recalled that 'the superficial Robertson' was an author still in use at Oxford when he was an undergraduate there in the 1840s. See Bentley 1993: 139.

> BOSWELL. 'Then, Sir, you would reduce all history to no better than an almanack, a mere chronological series of remarkable events.'
>
> Mr. Gibbon, who must at that time have been employed upon his history of which he produced the first volume in the following year, was present; but did not step forth in defence of that species of writing. He probably did not like to *trust* himself with JOHNSON!
>
> (Boswell 1791: II, 365–6)

Unlike most of his contemporaries, Gibbon believed he could recreate a past entire by paying attention to the known sources and discovering new ones in artefacts and the eighteenth-century mania for inscriptions. This determination, his talent for evocation and a prose of unsurpassed pointedness almost displaced him, indeed, from the model of representation that we are characterizing as an Enlightenment approach.

What kept him there was his irony: a Tacitean manner as *dix-huitième* as a tricorn hat.[14] The account works, as Gay points out, on at least two levels simultaneously. The public level of intention offered by his actors has one tone, the private reality a different one; 'he compels the reader to become his accomplice and to draw the unpleasant, generally cynical, inference for himself' (Gay 1975: 47). His sources never matched his creativity. Neither did the criticism that he brought to the ones he had. But he invented a text containing both meaning and explanation. The Romans lost their way by following courses and suffering adversities which would undermine any society and Gibbon's account of the undermining is conceived as a general explanation, not a particular one. He thinks, in other words, nomothetically; he explains the events by identifying the laws which govern them. There are many of these – the effeminacy generated by a lack of war, the unforeseen effects of economic exploitation, the weakness attending the expansion of empires, and so on. But one of them is critical and forms the subtext of the book as a whole. This lies in the contention that freedom is the guarantor of civic health – 'the happy parent taste and science' (Gibbon [1776–88] 1909: I, 64) – and its denial the harbinger of social sclerosis. Everything else follows. Not least, this means that government must avoid the pitfalls of crude democracy and remember that

> the firm edifice of Roman power was raised and preserved by the wisdom of ages. The obedient provinces of Trajan and the Antonines were united

---

14 On Gibbon's debt to Tacitus, see Gay 1975, esp. 26. Cf. Burrow 1985; Porter 1988.

by laws and adorned by arts . . . [T]he general principle of government was wise, simple and beneficent.'

(ibid. I, 31)

Yet of course Gibbon's starting-point is itself a derivative from that recent past on which enlightened opinion rested. His book celebrates implicitly the English constitutional settlement of 1689 and the freedom that it bestowed by chastising the Romans for having won the same prize and having lost it.

Through these books and less accomplished instances of an Enlightenment sensibility, the new historical values found expression. The importance for any critical form of enquiry of intellectual self-confidence and a rejection of metaphysical authority needs little argument; and to that extent the climate generated in Europe after 1750 contributed unquestionably to the development of historical ideas. It is less obvious how much it limited them. In generalizing its perceptions of a particular present and ironing out kinks in the human condition, eighteenth-century thought lost contact with the specific and the particular about which historians ultimately want to know. In reducing the world to law, the Enlightenment's understanding of history truncated the past as a domain for enquiry. It also became out of date virtually the moment it was announced. For the revolution of 1789 shattered more than French society, just as Napoleon's armies brought about the destruction of more than life and property. Dislocations across Europe gave rise to questions about the nature of states and the origins of cultural identity, about the *differences* between histories rather than their commonality. For philosophers as much as for historians, the world after 1789 called for something higher than cynicism, more memorable than the tattle of the *salon*, more plausible than the publicizing of progress and the hidden hand of *l'esprit humain*.

2

THE COUNTER-
ENLIGHTENMENT

All the glitter of Paris easily outshone a story of impending change east of the Rhine. Yet although that story lacked the gloss of the Enlightenment, it turned out to have more significance for the writing of history than what had taken place in France and Britain. The confused organism of principalities and potential states that would later coalesce as 'Germany' had begun to acquire its own voice by 1800. It was a timid voice at first. German intellectuals stood in awe of French achievement and culture. They copied British historiographical models drawn in particular from Hume, Robertson and Gibbon.[15] They shared a European fascination with Sir Walter Scott.[16] In the last third of the eighteenth century the German-speaking world nevertheless gave rise to the most talented array of intellectuals, artists and poets that has been squeezed into one or two generations in modern times: Goethe, Kant, Herder, Schiller, Hegel, Beethoven, Heine, Schubert. Some of their achievement ran parallel with the Enlightenment and fed on what others had sown. But more was original and, so far as the central characteristics of Enlightenment thought went, counter-thematic. In

---

15 See McClelland 1971: 13. For a recent magisterial survey of German intellectual currents, see Sheehan 1989, esp. chs 6 and 9.
16 For Scott, see Bann 1984. For Scott and Ranke, see Gilbert 1990: 37.

sharing Sir Isaiah Berlin's category of a 'Counter-Enlightenment' we are therefore calling attention to an important distinction rather than a frontal opposition.[17] We shall dwell on it, nevertheless, because no other intellectual initiative has played so great a role in fashioning attitudes to modern historical thinking.

Institutions played a considerable part in establishing a new understanding of history in Germany.[18] Two foundations – the University of Göttingen in 1737 and the new University of Berlin in 1810 – engage with the relevant events at a number of points. Göttingen became a point of entry for external, and especially British, ideas; and because it established the first historical school in Germany, the way opened for widespread reception of historical models from abroad. It generated, however, distinctive ideas of its own. Law and philology gained a status and collegiality with history which has since become a hallmark of German historical education (Breisach 1983; McClelland 1971: 16). They won that status not least because of the distinction of those appointed to teach. Looking back from the eve of the First World War, the historian G. P. Gooch (himself a sort of enlightened liberal) saw in Göttingen in the last part of the eighteenth century an unequalled academic community:

> While the new era of classical research is connected with Berlin, the historical study of jurisprudence is identified with Göttingen. Though Gesner and Heyne made the Hanoverian foundation the centre of philological studies for half a century, the political and historical sciences had always been strongly represented. Pütter in German law, Martens in International law, Spittler, Schlözer, Gatterer in history, Achenwall in statistics, formed a galaxy of which no other seat of learning could boast.
>
> (Gooch 1913: 42)

August Ludwig von Schlözer (1735–1809) concerned himself with translating Russian sources into German: a precondition for advances in German projects. But he also recommended against the current taste for the history of violence and war (*Mordgeschichte*) and believed that 'greater revolutions have often resulted from the quiet musings of

---

17 For explication of Berlin's views, see Gray 1995 and their polemical development in Gray's other recent writing.
18 I shall use the term 'Germany' as a convenient shorthand, despite the dangers of the term when referring to German history before 1871.

the genius and the gentle virtue of the man of wisdom than from the violence of all-powerful tyrants'.[19] Johann Christoph Gatterer (1727–99) considered the problems of method in history and in his work on diplomatic, numismatics and genealogy called attention to a variety of *Hilfswissenschaften*.[20]

In the case of Berlin, the circumstances of the university's foundation outweighed its intrinsic importance. The French Revolution had occasioned more alarm than admiration in Germany and the Napoleonic occupation had hardly lessened the concern. One result emerged in a new sense of Germanic nationalism, originally among the intelligentsia and later reflected in political and military elites. It comprised in effect the rejection of inferiority and asserted the claim to a history no less valuable than those of other cultures. Herder had argued in his *Reflections on the Philosophy of the History of Mankind* (1784–91) that the unit of analysis should be the *Volk*. The events around him persuaded him that it was time for the German people to see themselves as one of Europe's *Völker* and to look for their identity in the past. 'I do not believe,' he wrote in 1793, 'that the Germans have less feeling than other nations for the merits of their ancestors. I think I see a time coming when we shall return more seriously to their achievements and learn to value our old gold' (quoted in Gooch 1913: 54). It was in that spirit that national leaders such as vom Stein and intellectuals such as Humboldt put their weight behind the idea of a new university in Berlin: one that would act as a treasure house for the gold of the German past.

Certainly it would attract scholars in other areas too; one of Humboldt's first *coups* lay in enticing the gifted jurist Savigny to the new institution. But Stein's special interest explicitly comprised the German past and it was in this field that Berlin would prove particularly powerful. Stein had known the Danish bureaucrat Barthold Georg Niebuhr for some years. He brought Niebuhr to the University to develop his work in Roman history while acting as plenipotentiary for Prussia in discussions with Britain during the wars

---

19 Quoted in Reill 1975: 45. I am greatly indebted to Professor Reill's account in this section. Cf. Winter 1961.

20 For Gatterer and others, see the symposium 'Enlightenment Historiography: Three German Studies', *History and Theory*, Beiheft 11 (1971): 1–86.

of liberation. Niebuhr's achievement in his *History of Rome* (1811–12) would dominate Roman scholarship, as we shall see, until the work of Theodor Mommsen later in the century. But Stein wanted to go further than the classical period. He pressed for research and teaching in German history. One crucial outcome took shape in 1821. Under the guidance of an extraordinary archivist, Carl August Friedrich Pertz, a vast project to be called the *Monumenta Germaniae Historica* would identify, edit, annotate and print the dispersed record of the German people: its folk-tales, its literature, its charters, its manuscripts. Over a century and a half later that project still continues.[21] A further outcome had equally momentous consequences. In March 1825 the University appointed Leopold von Ranke to its teaching complement on the strength of his recently published history of early modern Europe from 1494 to 1535.[22] Over the next half-century he would introduce a revolution into the writing and teaching of history and give German history the self-confidence that Stein would have wished. Both in Ranke and more crudely in his pupils one can see a distinctive style of history running from the expulsion of Napoleon to the ascendancy of Kaiser Wilhelm:

> Out of the Wars of Liberation arose the myth of the Spirit of 1813 cultivated by Prussian-oriented historians from Droysen to Meinecke and central to the beliefs of the German historist[23] tradition. From this perspective the reformed Prussian monarchy marked a high point in the history of human freedom, a society in which the individual was fully free, but at the same time was integrated into a social whole. Here was the core of the 'German conception of freedom', of the ideas of 1813, which German historians contrasted sharply with the atomistic view of society supposedly inherent in the ideas of 1789.
>
> (Iggers 1983: 21)

This rejection of 'atomism' and the affirmation of 'historism' issued directly from the Counter-Enlightenment and they afford an instance

---

21 Perhaps one might note *en passant* that a French initiative in the wake of the *Monumenta* – the *Collections de documents inédits sur l'histoire de France* which began to appear from 1836 – owed its inspiration to Guizot and tried to achieve for France a similar objective to that reflected in Stein's project.

22 *Geschichten der romanischen und germanischen Völker von 1494 bis 1535* (1824), usually translated literally and dismally as the *Histories of the Latin and Teutonic Nations*.

23 The concept of 'historism' is discussed later in this book.

of how one cannot explain the nineteenth-century German experience in institutional terms alone. An important intellectual shift had plainly taken place and the new context makes little sense until one first understands it.

We have seen that Enlightenment history had claimed a status for itself as 'philosophical' to the extent that historical enquiry had a moral function, that of teaching by example. The German connection with philosophy rested on a firmer base. It took seriously the claim of historical writing to represent a sector of epistemology, i.e. it constituted a series of truth-claims about the past which required testing and validation in the same way as any other assertion of knowledge. For that reason the philosophies of Immanuel Kant, Johann Gottfried von Herder and G. W. F. Hegel assumed special significance for two generations of German students and teachers and it barely overstates the case to see the tenor of German historiography down to 1914 as having taken its character from a sympathy with, or aversion to, the cluster of philosophical positions often described as 'Idealist'.[24] To dwell on a difficult philosophical position may strike the reader as unnecessary when reviewing what historians wrote, but the contentions here will be that the view of the past constructed as a by-product of Idealist thought operated as an alternative assumption to that presented by the Enlightenment and that an adequate conception of nineteenth-century historiography will elude anyone who has not grasped that the argument wound between two poles and not around one of them.

Kant's spectacular achievement or disservice in *The Critique of Pure Reason* (1781) consisted in his separation of the real, existing world from the individual trying to make sense of it. For the divide envisaged by Kant between the 'knowing subject' (the observer) and his 'object' (the thing observed) was no trivial matter of distance or convenience or intelligence or disinformation. It derived from a fundamental and intractable truth. The 'knowing subject' gains his 'knowledge' of the world by processing internally the various kinds of sense-data available to him. But the data – the perfume of the flower, the taste of the sugar,

---

24 I shall use the capitalized form of the word to denote this philosophical meaning as opposed to the ascription of an elevated ethical position in politics or social thought that is normally connoted by lower-case idealism.

the image of the landscape – can never be transcended to give him knowledge of the thing that lay behind the bouquet, the taste and the perception. His 'knowledge' will never be more than an awareness of reality's effects on him; he can never transcend his body's confinements in order to investigate the external object – the *Ding-an-sich* or thing-in-itself – in the thing's own terms rather than the ones necessarily limiting his understanding. In so far as he claims 'knowledge' of reality, he is merely making a claim on behalf of pictures and sensory impressions gained of an external world which certainly exists and stimulates the impressions but which he can never know as he knows himself and his own thought-world.

If these ideas have any validity in thinking about the present world-in-itself, they presumably have no less force in contemplating the past world. Indeed, their urgency will increase because the very pastness which interests historians builds its own barriers against our finding out about it with the facility that we sometimes can bring to bear in the present. Kant himself did nothing to help his audience see the implications of his Idealism for historical enquiry. He wrote only one short essay about history[25] and, as in the case of David Hume, he leaves his philosophy behind the moment he thinks about 'old, half-effaced information from archives' (quoted in Beck 1963: vii) and writes like a Voltairean schoolboy. Others did see those implications, however, and the idea that the past does not exist (by definition) and that we can never *re*-construct it but only *construct* in our present a picture or image or model of it – one whose truth we can test only by its internal coherence with evidence rather than through a one-to-one correspondence with the erstwhile *Ding-an-sich* – we owe ultimately to Kant. It has proved a powerful strain in Western historical thought from his own day to our own through the writing of Dilthey, Croce, Collingwood and Oakeshott in contesting scientific models of understanding in Europe and that of Becker and Beard in dissolving superficial views of historical 'objectivity' in the United States.[26]

---

25 The tenor of Kant's writing on history can be gleaned from his essay 'Idea for a Universal History from a Cosmopolitan Point of View', printed in Beck 1963. For philosophical treatments of his historical ideas, see Galston 1975 and Yovel 1980.
26 On the latter movement, see Novick 1988, esp. 250–78. We do not have a synthetic

The tight rationalism of Kant's thought finds no reflection in Herder's chaotic system of speculation, but like Vico, with whom he bears close comparison (see Berlin 1976), Herder seems in retrospect an author marking a watershed in his recommendations over how the past must be understood. He reversed the Enlightenment's readiness to belittle cultures unlike its own by seeing that change over time was a crucial feature of how the world worked, that each *Volk* bore within itself the seeds of its own transformation which demanded a language of analysis relevant to its epoch and that it was pointless to criticize the classical world, for example, as though it were an apprentice version of the modern one. 'The Romans were precisely what they were capable of becoming; everything perishable belonging to them perished, and what was susceptible of permanence remained' (quoted in White 1973: 76). He does not remove reality from the observer, as Kant does. Rather he announces the principle that reality should be seen not as a state or a fixed given, but as a happening, a process of becoming through time. Both of his leading notions were to become part of historical thinking over the next century. His disavowal of anachronism and the suggestion that historians must conceive the subject in terms of the epoch studied gave impetus, in the absence of a still-neglected Vicoan approach, to the style of history that Friedrich Meinecke called *Historismus* or 'historism'. '[T]he essence of historism', he explained, 'is the substitution of a process of *individualising* observation for a *generalising* view of human forces in history . . . '. The whole process depended on breaking down the rigid ways of thought attached to the concepts of Natural Law

> and its belief in the invariability of the highest human ideals and an unchanging human nature that was held to be constant for all ages. . . . Only by a deeper understanding of the human soul could the old Natural Law and the new naturalism be transcended and a new sense of history achieved.[27]

overview of Idealist historical thought, though much suggestive material can be found in Jacobitti 1981, Ermarth 1978 and Liebel 1963/4. R. G. Collingwood is best approached through the posthumous compilation, *The Idea of History* (1946) and glossed in Mink 1969. Michael Oakeshott's formidable essay *On History* (1983) can be complemented by Goldstein 1976.

27 Meinecke 1972: IV, 3–4. It should be noted that 'historism' in Meinecke's sense is not only different from but contradictory to the predictive and determinist concept of

This determination to study the past for its own sake and in its own terms, rather than as a vehicle for generalization and law-building, dominated German historiography in the nineteenth century. The second formative idea – that reality must be sought in transformation – lies at the heart of Hegel's philosophy of history which gave rise to a cult following in the first half of the century and affected historians across Europe during the second.

For Hegel, the separation of man from his world seemed as intolerable as Kant's logic seemed impeccable. His system bridged the chasm by organizing reality as an evolving happening to which both mind and world contributed because – the end point of his complex metaphysics – mind and the world were joined together in a dialectical relationship which would ultimately show them to be the same reality differentiated by the abstractions of understanding. History was the story of this unfolding relationship and therefore had a special urgency for Hegel. He had no interest in empiricism, which would simply mislead because it lacked philosophical insight. History was centrally a philosophical activity which tracked the destiny of the world's mechanism which Reason had revealed. His students in the philosophy faculty of the University of Berlin found little to resemble the lectures of Niebuhr or the man who prided himself on his loathing for Hegel, Leopold von Ranke. Judging from their lecture-notes, from which the posthumous *Lectures on the Philosophy of History* were compiled, they found little intelligible at all. But the ascription to certain civilizations in the past of a functional role in the working out of an entire cosmology through the famous dialectic of thesis, antithesis, synthesis inspired those whose history had lost meaning under the logic-chopping of rationalism. Those, like Ranke, who hated it could not avoid it. Those who, like Nietzsche in the nineteenth or Spengler and Toynbee in the twentieth century, gravitated to a form of history which shaped the events of the past into a grand philosophical system worshipped implicitly at his shrine. Those who, like Marx, escaped the system by hijacking it and running it off in a new direction acquired a vehicle of enormous potential for transforming conceptions of how the past grew into the present.

'historicism' developed by Karl Popper in his *The Poverty of Historicism* (1957). In this discussion 'historist' will relate to Meinecke's sense, 'historicist' to Popper's.

Contrasting the Enlightenment mode of historical thinking in France and Britain with a Counter-Enlightenment persuasion in the German-speaking world has helped identify, then, twin poles of argument. Looking forward from 1800 it becomes possible now to discern clusters of historiography separated by those poles and the lines of force surrounding them. To the Enlightenment's influence we can readily trace the origins of a school, predominantly but not exhaustively French, that wished to see history as a social science. This is the world of Comte and Taine, of Fustel de Coulanges and Gabriel Monod, of Henry Thomas Buckle in England and a coterie of Americans. At the opposite end of the spectrum we shall discover a resistance to *Naturwissenschaft* as a key to historical method and the call for a distinctive *Geisteswissenschaft* which will acknowledge the autonomy of history as a human discipline, seeking forms of analysis and explanation quite foreign to the laboratory and the scientific journal. These will range from Macaulay and Carlyle on the British side, through Michelet on the French to several persuasions of writer by the end of the nineteenth century. And in the vacuum between these poles we shall discover Germany's greatest historian, owing allegiance to neither of their positions and transparently the victim of both.

3

ROMANTICISM

The competing persuasions available to historical thinkers and writers by the turn of the nineteenth century did not confine themselves to their own territories, insulated from world events. They co-mingled and drew both strength and opposition from events taking place 'on the ground'. Among the most significant determinants after 1815 was the defeat of revolutionary sentiment and its further repression in England; a period of intense rethinking of the recent past in France by a generation needing to accommodate the enormities of the Revolution, the Directorate and Napoleon; and the birth of a new American sensibility, fresh from its second defeat of the British in 1814 and finding an historical version of itself that would reflect the uniqueness of the American venture. To make all these projects sound the same stretches credibility and does little justice to the singularities of each. Yet since we are searching for intellectual environments in which to locate the writing of history, there remains some point in grouping together forms of writing which their authors would never have grouped, using the retrospect which they manipulated with some distinction in their histories but which was denied to them when they tried to understand their own location just as we struggle to make sense of ours. Grouping invites categories and perhaps the idea of 'romanticism' does less violence to these histories than might some alternatives.

Romantic historiography took its focus and its audience in resistance to the cold and clinical perspectives associated with rationalism. Not that it abandoned evidence or wanted to see historical accounts reduced to hagiography: many of the Romantics held a sophisticated view of the relationship between evidence and text and criticized their Enlightenment predecessors for behaving in a cavalier spirit when faced with stubborn facts. None of them expressed that criticism more cuttingly than Thomas Babington Macaulay in his evisceration of Hume in 1828. It is true that Hume's 'Tory' credentials upset Macaulay's Whig ones but the ammunition used by the latter concerned the technical question of evidence and argument rather than Hume's political drift:

> Without positively asserting much more than he can prove, he gives prominence to all the circumstances which support his case; he glides lightly over those which are unfavourable to it; his own witnesses are applauded and encouraged; the statements which seem to throw discredit on them are controverted; the contradictions into which they fall are explained away; a clear and connected abstract of their evidence is given. Everything that is offered on the other side is scrutinised with the utmost severity; every suspicious circumstance is a ground for comment and invective; what cannot be denied is extenuated or passed by without notice; concessions even are sometimes made; but this insidious candour only increases the effect of the vast mass of sophistry.
>
> (Macaulay [1828] 1956: 81)

Rather than attempt to beat the Enlightenment at its own game, the Romantics sought to transcend the world of flat, nomological reportage and to produce a history that was creative and alive and the reverse of value-free. Some of them – a very few – had read Vico. More of them had come into contact with German literature and conceived an admiration for Goethe or Schiller. Most of them had discovered in Savigny and Niebuhr models of how to undertake rigorous enquiry. Where they went further was in their understanding of how an historical text should look and what a reader would gain from it. They addressed consciously what Gibbon had achieved on the run – the need to hold attention and keep a reader reading. They chose to make history learn from literature and to function in the same way. It would have the captivation produced by a Waverley novel and its illumination of reality would operate through broadly the same mechanisms that Scott employed. Its truth would be poetic and not merely expository. Its method would embrace intuition as much as analysis; its explanations would turn on the particularities of persons, the unrepeatability of events.

All of this would work itself out against the background of revolution, liberty and repression. The events of 1789 and again of 1830 affected romantic historians in a central and inescapable way; and when those revolutions turned to counter-revolutions, history became the torch that liberals might carry in defiance. 'The liberal historians of the restoration [in France]', one scholar recently judged,

> rescued the pre-revolutionary past. What took place after 1830 amounted to a reordering, a recomposition of the national tradition. Michelet went beyond the views of Guizot, Mignet and Thierry and wrote what his contemporaries called symbolic history, an interpretative narrative in which events were related to the unfolding of a more general purpose. He felt he was lending his voice to the people, that he was speaking on behalf of the masses whom previous historians had condemned to silence. National history was related to the patterns of universal history. The Revolution was situated within the vaster continuity of world, even cosmic history.
>
> (Crossley 1993: 42–3)

A full understanding of these authors, most of whom had been born just after the French Revolution and who had grown up during the 1810s and 1820s, requires an acknowledgement of how conscious and contrived was this search for poetic expression through the medium of reviviscence and at what level the search took place. To see them as practitioners of no more than a 'florid rhetorical style' for 'readers who seek entertainment rather than instruction' misses their purpose and substitutes an inappropriate test for them to fail.[28] When Carlyle deemed it 'part of [his] creed that the only Poetry is History, could we tell it right' (quoted in Rosenberg 1985: 48), he voiced an aspiration fundamental to romantic historical thought and showed why an obsession with how to write history books figured so generally in this genre. The text had to carry the same ontological weight as a poem. If its language carried beyond the conversational, so did its message; and it is therefore less than intelligent to criticize Macaulay or Carlyle or Michelet for an over-rich style: one might as well seek to diminish

---

28 Barnes 1963: 232, 190 alluding respectively to Carlyle and George Bancroft. Of the latter, Barnes writes engagingly that '[t]he damage done to sane perspective in American history by his works was almost incalculable, if not irreparable' (232).

Keats or Coleridge or Emerson or Thoreau for the same reason. Like poetry, moreover, romantic history was afflicted by structure and the question how best to arrange the writing to make its point tell. On this issue the studies taking their moment of origin in the period from 1830 to 1850 suggest a complete unanimity. The vehicle of romantic history was narrative; but it asked for imagination beyond the putting of events in chronological order along the lines that the eighteenth century had so frequently thought adequate. It began with the criticism that the Enlightenment and its disciples had 'miserably neglect[ed] the art of narration, the art of interesting the affections and presenting pictures to the imagination'. (Macaulay [1828] 1956: 83). Only a skilful narrative would have the literary power to delineate truths about liberty and the congealing of peoples into new formations that this generation wanted to portray. Besides, narrative had an explanatory value in talking about processes, perhaps in talking about anything at all. 'Cut us off from Narrative', Carlyle intoned, 'how would the stream of conversation, even among the wisest, languish into detached handfuls, and among the foolish utterly evaporate!' (Carlyle [1830] 1956: 91).

Poetic truth and narrative method brought another impulse: the need to silhouette the guiding historical personality, the luminous moment of action. The purpose of the story lies in taking the reader to an ocean-floor of ultimate reality but on reaching it he or she rarely discovers large structures or geological formations. One is taught to think about collectivities as agglommerations of tiny individuals and as existing only in and through them. There exists a world of the social – indeed Michelet has some claim to have been the first to develop it – but we are never allowed to forget that history is 'the essence of innumerable biographies'. This environment is one where heroes and heroines flourish and have meaning which historians must identify and exhibit. The licence does not stop at writing lives of unpleasant tyrants, as Voltaire did; it encompasses the presentation of individuals in a positive light as bearers of the *Zeitgeist* or beacons of hope. They might be great leaders, as Carlyle made Cromwell or Frederick the Great. They might be faceless members of the crowd milling about the guillotine, a constant presence in Michelet's history of the French Revolution but, as Owen Chadwick cautions, never a social force or movement in the modern sense because writing that turns on individuals knows no movement, only the agents whose several efforts might be so labelled. 'Though he wrote of the crowd, the crowd was to him a collection of free individuals, each of whom he would describe if he could' (Chadwick 1975: 198). This thought serves all the Romantics. They each tried to describe every person, every thought, every action, every horse, every tree. The practicalities of text and source, nothing else, hindered them. For the work was inspired by the drive to evoke and make present by an effort of imagination and will.

Carlyle (1795–1881) and Macaulay (1800–59) sprang from the same generation as Michelet but the particularities of their Scottish and English backgrounds naturally franked their divergent careers and impact. Undoubtedly the Scotland of Annandale and Edinburgh marked Carlyle's imaging and expression, though in his case the importation of Schiller, whose life he wrote, and German philosophy had equal effect. Between them, these conflicting tensions produced an approximation to a prophet rather than a social commentator and a prose style that the twentieth century cannot tolerate for more than a couple of sentences. His two central works of history, if one disregards a poor edition of Cromwell's letters and speeches, were *The French Revolution* of 1833–42 and his life of *Frederick the Great* (1858–65). Both of them held a major place in British historiography in the nineteenth century until the urge towards a 'scientific' historiography began to redraw the priorities in the 1860s. The quality that most guaranteed their success lay in their pictorial character. Carlyle fills the mind with images which, once created, do not leave it. One of the most startling and permanent surrounded his account of the execution of Robespierre, following the suicide attempt that had blasted his jaw, at the end of volume three of *The French Revolution* and it may stand for others in its theatrical sliding of tense, the familiarity of Christian-name terms with the actors, the repetition of adjective and noun to deepen atmosphere, the near-physical sense of presence so that the reader's own moment becomes the afternoon of 28 July 1794.

> At four in the afternoon, never before were the streets of Paris seen so crowded. From the Palais de Justice to the Place de la Révolution, for *thither* again go the Tumbrils this time, it is one dense stirring mass; all windows crammed; the very roofs and ridge-tiles budding forth human Curiosity, in strange gladness. The Death-tumbrils, with their motley Batch of Outlaws, some Twenty-three or so, from Maximilien

[Robespierre], to Mayor Fleuriot and Simon the Cordwainer, roll on. All eyes are on Robespierre's Tumbril, where he, his jaw bound in dirty linen, with his half-dead Brother and half-dead Henriot, lie shattered. . . . At the foot of the scaffold, they stretched him out on the ground till his turn came. Lifted aloft his eyes again opened; caught the bloody axe. Samson wrenched the coat off him; wrenched the dirty linen from his jaw: the jaw fell powerless, there burst from him a cry; – hideous to hear and see. Samson, thou canst not be too quick!

Samson's work done, there bursts forth shout on shout of applause. Shout, which prolongs itself not only over Paris, but over France, but over Europe, and down to this generation.[29]

The *Führerprinzip* of his later years did nothing to help Carlyle's popularity, especially in his encomium on Frederick the Great who, for all his undoubted success, looked neither like an 1848 revolutionary nor an 1858 Palmerstonian.

To many it appears certain there are to be no Kings of any sort, no Government more; less and less need of them henceforth, New Era having come. Which is a very wonderful notion; important if true; perhaps still more important, just at present, if untrue! My hopes of presenting, in this Last of the Kings, an exemplar to my contemporaries, I confess, are not high.[30]

Yet Carlyle's hold is all too easily minimized in modern recollection. One does well to recall a figure like James Anthony Froude who, though his own historical work went in very different directions, retained always his sense of overwhelming indebtedness to Carlyle's example. 'Carlyle to me spoke as never man spoke . . . [I]n all that I thought or attempted, I allowed his judgement to guide me.'[31]

Despite his lionization in Cheyne Row in his later years, Carlyle never reached the inner core of Britain's governing classes. Macaulay was born in it. Having a father who had held a diplomatic post as governor of Sierra Leone gave one a certain start in life: and Zachary

---

29 Thomas Carlyle, *The French Revolution* (3 vols, 1833–42), III, 242–3. For a full analysis of his method in this text, cf. Sorenson 1983.
30 *History of Friedrich II of Prussia, called Frederick the Great* (8 vols, 1858–65, 1897 edn, I, 16–17). Carlyle's shade would not have been amused when H. D. Traill forgave him in the Gladstonian edition of 1897 on the ground that he probably did not believe what he wrote (xiii–xiv).
31 Dunn 1961–3: I, 210–12. Recent studies of Carlyle and his impact include Le Quesne 1982 and Campbell 1993.

Macaulay's son in his turn had a professional career that looked like Gibbon's: Member of Parliament, cabinet office in Melbourne's government.[32] But of course historians are more interested in his *History of England* (5 vols, 1849–61), which remained unfinished at his death and had, indeed, paid the price of all narrative by never getting further than the reign of William III, despite an original intention to come down to 1830.[33] Like Hume, he achieved a major *succès d'estime*. But he did much else like Hume, for all the waspish words of his essay on how to write history. He celebrated the Glorious Revolution backwards, when he wrote about the period before 1688, and forwards when he looked ahead of it. He needled the Church because it stood in the way of liberty; but then he attacked everything so defined. He wrote some of the greatest paragraphs ever composed about the history of England as well as some of the silliest and some (more tellingly) that Hume could have written himself. Note the supposed reception of General Monk's declaration for a free Parliament:

> As soon as his declaration was known, the whole nation was wild with delight. Wherever he appeared thousands thronged round him, shouting and blessing his name. The bells of all England rang joyously: the gutters ran with ale; and night after night, the sky five miles round London was reddened by innumerable bonfires.
>
> (Macaulay 1849: I, 128)

It hardly mattered. Macaulay turned history into a rival for the three-decker novel and quite overcame among the booksellers the careful scholarship of a Thomas Arnold or Henry Hart Milman. Perhaps these 'Liberal Anglicans' had the making of a new historical method (see Forbes 1952, *passim*), but it was Macaulay who reached the readers. The sales of the first two volumes, which came out in 1849, had been

---

32 Macaulay sat in the House of Commons for the Whig interest in 1830–4, 1839–47 and 1852–6. He held government office as secretary for war from 1839 to 1841 and paymaster-general in Russell's government in 1846–7.

33 'How far I shall bring the narrative down I have not determined. The death of George the Fourth would be the best halting place. The history would then be an entire view of all the transactions which took place between the revolution, which brought the crown into harmony with the parliament, and the revolution which brought the parliament into harmony with the nation' (Macaulay to Macvey Napier, 20 July 1838, quoted in Millgate 1973: 125). Had he continued at the density suggested by his account of the Restoration and Revolution, the project would have taken twenty volumes to complete.

striking enough in Britain. In America they sold 200,000 sets in the first year.

Not that America lacked a historiography of its own: indeed in George Bancroft (1800–91) it had discovered possibly its first major historian and another witness to the Romantic persuasion. As a son of religious Dissent in Massachusetts he reflected the provincialism of Carlyle. In everything else he echoed Macaulay. Although he tried Harvard for a short period on his return from studying in Germany, he disliked the environment and did not succeed in it. Schoolteaching came no more easily. He found his *métier* through holding government positions and maintaining an active political life while writing his ten-volume *History of the United States*. Like Macaulay he was a Whig, though one understood in its American sense; he later became a Democrat. His dovetailing into the emerging American state went quite as far as Macaulay's into the British. He played a role in nominating Polk for the presidency. He served as Polk's Secretary of the Navy in 1845–6, the year before Macaulay joined Russell's government. Then Polk made him ambassador to Britain, so he met Macaulay and Milman and Hallam and other celebrated figures in the British historical establishment. After the Civil War his affinities with Andrew Johnson led to his appointment at Berlin where his acquaintances ran from Bismarck and Moltke at one end of the spectrum to Ranke and Mommsen at the other.

But Bancroft's intellectual contacts turned out the more significant. Unusually for one of his generation, he studied at Göttingen after completing his first degree at Harvard and then moved around Berlin and elsewhere, attending courses by Hegel and Schleiermacher in Berlin, spending time with Goethe at Weimar. He thus felt the full weight of Counter-Enlightenment thought but carried it only as a form of Christian optimism and liberal triumphalism which marked his historical work throughout a long career of writing. Coupled with immersion in the state (the *fons et origo* of so much romantic thought), his uplift produced narratives of remarkable simplicity of view. He saw social history working itself out in the state-order and in the special order produced by Americans. Even a work from late in his life on the history of the constitution contains the plenitude of thankfulness that would irritate the generation of Beard and Harry Elmer Barnes beyond description. Consider his very first paragraph:

The order of time brings us to the most cheering act in the political history of mankind, when thirteen republics . . . formed themselves into one federal commonwealth. There was no revolt against the past, but a persistent and healthy progress. The sublime achievement was the work of a people led by statesmen of earnestness, perseverance, and public spirit, instructed by the widest experience in the forms of representative government, and warmed by that mutual love which proceeds from ancient connection, harmonious effort in perils, and common aspirations.

(Bancroft 1882: I, 3)

Six hundred and fifty pages later, as we come to the end of his story, the mood has not altered. '[A] new people had risen up without king, or princes, or nobles' and had written for themselves a constitution which they might almost have found dictated on Sinai.

In the happy morning of their existence as one of the powers of the world, they had chosen justice for their guide; and while they proceeded on their way with a well-founded confidence and joy, all the friends of mankind invoked success for their endeavour as the only hope for renovating the life of the civilized world.

(ibid. II, 367)

Though Bancroft had spent a little time in Paris it seems that Jules Michelet (1798–1874) remained one of the very few notables in Europe whom he never met. It was just as well: their democratic impulses ran divergently. Michelet lacked Bancroft's cosmopolitanism, though his missionary work on behalf of Vico suggested that he wanted to do more than magnify France.[34] Yet Michelet's achievement lay so close to a vision of the French people's achievement that the two do not readily separate. The involvement with the state so evident in the other writers we have discussed is not replicated here, except negatively when Michelet was sacked from his position as keeper of the national archives at the restoration as a reprisal for having welcomed the revolution of 1848. Unlike the others he held academic positions: he had been a professor of ancient history at the *Ecole Normale* before moving to the *Archives* in 1831. Rather than silhouette the recent French state as an embodiment of liberality (as a Macaulay or Bancroft might have done), Michelet's version of democracy made him face the other way and conceive a different trajectory – one that had its rise but also its fall.

---

34 See Michelet 1833, which has a 'Discourse sur le système et la vie de Vico'.

The reason takes little finding. Behind him Michelet had at half a century's remove the most spectacular revolution of the modern world, one in which he identified the French soul. He had no 1688 or 1776 since when the world had grown better and better. He had 1789 since when the world had retarded into the mediocrity and compromise of the empire which even the eruptions of 1830 and 1848 had failed to avert. And he had predecessors like Mignet who had already plotted a path towards welcoming the Revolution.[35] Like Carlyle, he could not baptize the results of Whig complacency. Unlike him, he found no pleasure in blaming the people. Michelet therefore presents a parabola to the retrospect of France and his commentators do not readily forgive him the excesses which he displays in conceiving of a period of greatness followed by a collapse into a diseased state. For Gooch, half a century later, the disease was not France's but Michelet's: we have the first six volumes of his early *History of France* rated as his 'most perfect and enduring work . . . written before his genius had reached its fullest development and before his imagination had become diseased' (Gooch 1913: 178). But *The French Revolution* shows him in decline: a peddler of disgusting scandal, incest and unwholesomeness. One sees what Gooch had in mind. But he misses the point that for Michelet France had been wrong in failing to seize the day; she had fallen away from the highest of ideals and succumbed to restoration through the human frailties that he narrates. Even the frailest – Danton and especially Robespierre – he loved with a passion that left him bereft on completing the book.[36]

Yet Hayden White's brilliant investigation of the innerness of Michelet's volumes substantiates an alternative view: that the sense

---

35 'Long before Michelet, Mignet's work struck many as preaching both the acceptance of the whole Revolution and the acceptance of the *necessity* for the whole Revolution' (Ben-Israel 1968: 61).

36 His widow published in 1888 a fragment in which he grieves for his loss. 'Le plus grand vide à cette table de bois blanc, d'où mon livre s'en va maintenant et où je reste seul, c'est de n'y plus voir mon pâle compagnon, le plus fidèle de tous, qui, de 89 en thermidor, ne m'avait point quitté; l'homme de grande volunté, laborieux comme moi et pauvre comme moi, avec qui, chacque matin, j'eus tant d'âpres [bitter] discussions. Le plus grand fruit de mon étude morale, physiologique, c'est justement cette dispute, c'est d'avoir serieusement anatomisé Robespierre' *Histoire de la révolution française* (2 vol. edn, Paris, 1952), II, 995).

of disease and corruption after 1789 inhered in Michelet's historical judgement which went far beyond the sources that he brought into play. This going beyond is what gives Michelet the sense of romance as well as the touch of greatness as an artist. His listening for 'words that were never spoken' and determination to 'make the silences of history speak' (see White 1973: 158) turn him all too readily into a spokesman for unborn *annalistes* or into some proto-Derrida. He sits more naturally, perhaps, with a volume of Romantic poetry or a canvas by Delacroix. On the other hand, he represents the ambiguities of romance in the period when it had become uncomfortable. If Michelet did not study in Göttingen and Berlin, his source-criticism suggested that German method had not been lost on the French. If his intellect made him the French Vico and his passion the French Carlyle, he had done enough in his excavation of national archives to pass muster as the French Ranke.

4

RANKE

Romance had not escaped the Germans. They applied it, however, to a culture that had a past but little history. To read their rediscovered *Volk* backwards into the blurredest origins in folk-tale plainly acted as an important imperative and it produced new histories of a peculiar (and to the modern ear all too familiar) kind. So we find the nine volumes of Voigt's *History of Prussia* dedicated 'To the Fatherland'[37] or one stumbles over Luden and his 'wish that we Germans would study like children the life of our beloved parents, dominated by the holy thought of the Fatherland.'[38] Compared with the great narratives created in England, France and America, such work nevertheless made little impact outside Germany: the romantic form found more authentic expression in poetry, music and the philosophy of the spirit. Instead, the main line of German historiography discovered an antidote to intuition in theorizing about historical method. Humboldt's lecture 'On the Tasks of the Historian' (1821) talks in a sophisticated way about history's function of finding form within chaos, of designating events

---

37 'The supreme prize in research is when the spirit is raised to reverence and the heart is filled with enthusiasm at the sight of great and good men.' (see Gooch 1913: 73).

38 Heinrich Luden (1778–1847). The remark comes from his lectures at Jena in 1808, quoted in Gooch 1913: 72. His *magnum opus* was to be a *History of the German People* (12 vols, 1825–37).

as parts of organic wholes, of going deeper than the flow of occurrence in order to locate in some more fundamental sense the 'form of history per se'.[39] A second prophylactic against intuition already existed, of course, in the source-based *œuvres* of figures such as Niebuhr and Eichhorn[40] whose thrust lay in protecting the intellect from romantic subversion rather than encouraging its attack on the 'march of mind' in the manner of Carlyle. Together, these elements helped promote an approach to history which we associate inevitably with its greatest emblem – Leopold von Ranke – but which has dimensions larger than Ranke's own contribution and amounts to a cultural identity.

Georg Iggers has analysed that identity through a lifetime's reflection on the distinctiveness of German historicism and it may be helpful to summarize his central findings (Iggers 1983). Most obviously in the century of Ranke, Droysen, von Sybel, Treitschke and a mass of lesser-known apologists for the *Machtstaat*, one can see a pervasive concern with the state, not only as an agency of authority domestically and power externally but as an ethical end in itself. Second, ethics become a product of that theatre of action which history considers. German historians reject the imposition of an ethical code from above the events and allow the events to announce their own morality. What ought to succeed becomes a function of what has succeeded – a doctrine with direct implications for the foregoing theory of the state. Third, one needs to be aware of historism, an agreement that historical knowledge will not emerge by applying conceptual schemata to the past but only through the analysis of individual instances and concrete events. To these guidelines we should, perhaps, add a fourth. German historical thinking did not remain static during the nineteenth century. It becomes important, therefore, to distinguish styles of thought prevalent between 1820 and 1870 from those that were to gain ascendancy between the foundation of the Empire and the cataclysm of 1914. In the first half of that period, for example, German historians made much of a supposed affinity with

---

39 Wilhelm von Humboldt, *On the Tasks of the Historian* (1821), quoted in White 1973: 180. For a study of Humboldt in English, see Sweet 1978–80.

40 Karl Friedrich Eichhorn ranks with Savigny as an interpreter of the history of German public and private law. See his *Deutsche Staats- und Rechtsgeschichte* (3rd edn, 1821–3).

the British: they often visited England, as Ranke himself did.[41] In the later decades the Wilhelmine historians turned in on themselves and generated a distaste abroad which the First World War seemed to confirm and which convicted all German historians of views held by a few of a particular generation. This helps explain why no new edition of Ranke's work appeared in Britain or France until the 1960s.[42]

Yet Ranke's date of birth – he was born in Thuringia in 1795 – ought in itself to exonerate him from allegations of this kind. Indeed only his amazing longevity colludes with them, for had he died before 1871 he might never have been associated with the imperial spirit. His classical education and formative years as a historian during the 1820s took place outside a formalized state system, though his admiration for Prussia – reinforced in 1831 by his return to Berlin from his work in the Italian archives – left a permanent mark on his idea of political history. Thereafter the prodigious output and swings of mood left behind him a range of history so vast that it confutes any notion of *précis* and presents all students of his work with an unclimbable mountain. The image of his sitting in old age editing the first forty-five volumes of his own writing is enough by itself to loosen any serious grasp on the part of a general reader, unless he or she elevates Ranke to an obsession quite as pronounced as the one he made of the history of Europe between the Renaissance and the French Revolution. Even in old age he foxed those who knew him well. Lord Acton looked back in 1895 on their last meeting:

> I saw him last in 1877, when he was feeble, sunken, and almost blind, and scarcely able to read or write. He uttered his farewell with kindly emotion, and I feared that the next I should hear of him would be the news of his death. Two years later, he began a Universal History, which is not without traces of weakness, but which, composed after the age of eighty-three, and carried, in seventeen volumes, far into the Middle Ages, brings to a close the most astonishing career in literature.[43]

In order to penetrate the sheer mass of this material, we need to ask questions about at least four of its aspects: its epistemology or view of

---

41 For the relationship with Britain, see McClelland 1971.
42 See Leopold von Ranke, *The Theory and Practice of History*, ed. G. G. Iggers and Konrad von Moltke (Indianapolis, 1973), xvii. In the United States after 1918 the distaste assumed more strident proportions: cf. Novick, 1988: 140–4.
43 Inaugural lecture at Cambridge, quoted in McNeill 1967: 336.

historical knowledge; its idea of historical understanding; its doctrines about explanation; and its implications about method. And with Ranke quite as much as with the context of his work, we shall need to be sensitive about change over time. The man who confronted the universe at the age of 83 was not the one who attracted an offer from the University of Berlin with his *History of the Latin and Teutonic Peoples* of 1825.

Two celebrated remarks take one close to the centre of Ranke's position on historical knowledge. The preface to the *Latin and Teutonic Peoples* contains the now notorious injunction to reconstruct the past 'wie es eigentlich gewesen'. The need to say what 'really' happened encouraged an entire branch of historiography – the American – to persist with its cult of objectivity.[44] It also misread Ranke's intention. The word 'eigentlich' had a nineteenth-century connotation resembling the English word 'essentially'; but when Ranke used it he seems to have had in mind a literal meaning – not 'mainly' or 'preponderantly' or 'in outline', but rather 'in essence', a term he used repeatedly. 'We . . . desire to root tradition in our knowledge of actual existence,' he wrote to his brother in 1838, 'and in our insight into its essence.'[45] Because that essence lies below a number of surfaces, moreover, the historian can never reach it through the mere adducing of evidence; in fact he rarely reaches it at all. Hence the second *bon mot*: 'Man bemüht sich, man strebt, am Ende hat man's nicht erreicht' – one tries and strains, but in the end one has not achieved that entering into the essence of the past which is the point of historical effort.[46] More accurate than a sense of Ranke's composition as a form of unthinking *pointillisme* is therefore one that depicts him as a frustrated van Gogh, never quite able to render the mimesis authentic. The thought also gives the lie to Ranke's scientific empiricism and supposed rejection of conceptual views.[47]

---

44 This misunderstanding has been clearly identified by Iggers: see his *The German Conception of History* (1983).

45 Ranke to Ferdinand von Ranke, 9 Aug. 1838, quoted in Krieger 1977: 37. It will be obvious how much this section owes to Professor Krieger's elucidations of Ranke's texts.

46 See Gilbert 1990: 36. The quotation also comes from the preface to the *Latin and Teutonic Peoples*.

47 Krieger 1977 argues persuasively for a distinction between Ranke's 'method of

His understanding owed more to Herder and Hegel than he himself allowed. His division of Western civilization into Latin and Teutonic types proved only the beginning of an analysis of European peoples along the lines of language and among categories of *Völker* which are then dovetailed into the state system and the emergent balance of power which comments on the ethical virility of the states involved in it.[48] When he thinks about the heart of the impulse towards modernity, he points to an individual or national mind in preference to armies; and on numerous occasions Ranke sounds as though he were a pupil of Hegel more than a critic, as when he speaks of 'the profound necessity of the inner course of things' or sees '[e]very power . . . moved by the inherent drive of the ideas lying at its base'.[49] The difference lay in the relationship envisaged between particular events and the generalizations which Ranke made to embrace them. He reads the unique and the common as working in tension rather than complementing one another in the synthetic process envisaged by Hegel. 'On the *opposition* of the particular and the general all European history is based.'[50] That sense of generality had entered Ranke's writing from the later part of his *History of the Popes* (1840), for all the detailed examination of events and personalities in that archival *tour de force*, and he defined it there not merely as the general context within which historians have to situate events in order to understand them but also as a style of history in its own right showing 'the inner changes of the spiritual-earthly tendencies of the world as they appear from epoch to epoch'.[51] These inner changes form the kernel of his study of *German History in the Age of the Reformation* (1839–52) and his comparative accounts of France and England in the seventeenth century (Ranke 1852–6; 1859–69).

---

knowledge', where he is interested in particulars, and his 'substance of knowledge', where he seeks universal truths – leaving him with 'an operational solution for a problem which he left unresolved in its own theoretical terms' (1977: 15).

48 See the very helpful exploration of these themes in White 1973: 176ff.

49 These remarks come from the late 1840s and 1850s when Ranke is portrayed by Krieger as undergoing a 'second synthesis' in the development of his ideas: see Krieger 1977: 202–45.

50 From a private lecture to King Maximilian, 1850s: ibid. 241. (emphasis added).

51 Ranke to Ritter, Feb./Nov. 1835, quoted in Krieger 1977: 152.

Understanding Ranke's overall vision is especially important because he has traditionally struck students of historiography as deserving their attention for his having been the father of a method. He used primary sources in archives with a zest and thoroughness quite new to historical scholarship. He taught his students by making them read primary sources under his guidance: the origin of the 'special subject' in the university curriculum and the beginning of the 'seminar', albeit of a kind very different from those operating today. Both of these novelties in research and teaching had the most far-reaching consequences and historians of education have a strong case in dwelling on them. But one misses too easily the part of Ranke that had little claim to scientific method: the pre-archival mind that brought its own structures to bear on the material. In this sense Ranke had close affinities with the Romantic historiography that he wanted to disown because his very mode of constituting his thousands of pages of text had implications that he could not discern:

> What Ranke did not see was that one might well reject a Romantic approach to history in the name of objectivity, but that, as long as history was conceived to be *explanation by narration*, one was required to bring to the task of narration the archetypal myth or plot structure, by which alone that narrative could be given a form. . . . His objectivity, critical principles, and sympathy for all sides of the conflicts he encountered through the historical record were deployed within the sustaining atmosphere of a metahistorical prefiguration of the historical field as a set of conflicts that must necessarily end in harmonious resolutions, resolutions in which 'nature' is finally supplanted by 'society' that is as just as it is stable.[52]

Ranke believed that the Prussia of his day embodied that just and stable society. He rejoiced in the loss of momentum of revolutionary ideas quite as much as Michelet grieved over them. In explaining the past, his problem lay simply in finding the generalizations – they seem often to work as historical laws – that joined together a fragmented and unhappy past with an organic and satisfactory present.

All these characteristics lend Ranke his distinctive voice in German historiography in the first half of the nineteenth century. It goes

---

52 White 1973: 167. The implications of White's views about the nature of narrative are further discussed in two collections of his essays: *Tropics of Discourse: Essays in Cultural Criticism* (1980), and *The Content of the Form: Narrative Discourse and Historical Representation* (1987). For a recent philosophical treatment, see *Ricœur* 1984–8.

without saying that there were other voices, some of them as powerful as Ranke's. His pupil Georg Waitz (1813–86) developed at Göttingen techniques of *Verfassungsgeschichte* or constitutional history that some have seen as superior to Ranke's in their precision.[53] His younger contemporary, Theodor Mommsen (1817–1903), has many claims to standing closer to the centre of a 'German school' in its supposed acknowledgement of a historical 'science' and through his prosecution of Roman history on a Rankean scale. (His *curriculum vitae* is supposed to have contained 1,500 publications.) Certainly these and other German authors will make their presence felt later in this account. What has helped focus attention on Ranke at this point is a collection of characteristics that make him relevant to our theme. He was the most self-conscious writer of history in the modern age; he consequently reflects helpfully on the climates of opinion around him. He has attracted a battery of modern criticism and exegesis because of that reflection, so we can gain closer access to him than would be possible for others. He manifests, most importantly, his generation's ambiguities about thought and method. Where those ambiguities disappear, he loses them in God. He places events under God's hand and sees in their tendency God's moving finger. In that respect he points not forwards but backwards. Those historians who were not convinced Lutherans like Ranke had come to fear by 1840 that God, too, had become ambiguous.

---

53 He undertook a great deal of editing of sources for the Monumenta but the large-scale original works are *Deutsche Verfassungsgeschichte* (1844–78) and *Deutsche Kaiser von Karl dem Grossen bis Maximilian* (1864).

5

THE VOICE OF SCIENCE

Ranke's Lutheranism, Arnold's Anglicanism and Bancroft's Congregationalism form elements in a common sensibility through the 1820s and 1830s. Theirs was the last generation for whom divine guidance and intervention remained obvious and crucial aspects of historical explanation. Even within that generation, however, notable inroads had already been made. The development of classificatory science associated with Linnaeus (1707–78), Buffon (1707–88) and Lamarck (1744–1829) made available a new descriptive vocabulary which could transcend that of orthodox Christianity less by opposing than ignoring it. Some could even see the two things as entwined, science as the godfather of religion. 'The reading of *histories*, my dear Sir,' Samuel Taylor Coleridge addressed his audience,

> may dispose a man to satire; but the science of HISTORY – History studied in the light of philosophy, as the great drama of an ever-unfolding Providence has a very different effect. It infuses hope and reverential thoughts of man and his destination.
>
> (Coleridge [1830] 1976: 32)

From mid-century the new language gained currency from the work of Charles Darwin and Alfred Russel Wallace with highly significant results in the 1870s and 1880s. Seen as a whole, indeed, the nineteenth century saw a process of 'secularization' within the Western intelligentsia which brooked no denial.[54] In the case of its historians, on the other hand, we need to exercise care for the rush towards the secular in this sector by no means reflected that discovered among those committed to various forms of 'social science'. Geographically it lacked all symmetry: French and American historians made more of it, for example, than the British. Indeed one could make a case for British singularity in witnessing a surprising persistence of religious category and assumption as the basis of its historiography (see Bentley 1993). Nor did the 'scientific' impetus carry the same message to all parts of Europe. In France it became, for a time, a cult of generalization about historical method. In Germany it advanced a new school of economic history. In Britain it has to be sought, as ever, in a subtle change of climate that is better associated with the forensic work of an extraordinary collection of medievalists than with those who wanted to turn the world upside down. Yet for all those differences of emphasis, the spread of scientific language and method exercised a compelling influence in making the second half of the century very different from the first.

France provided much impetus for the new approach. The scientific approach to documentation that we associate with Germany had made its mark in France also through the efforts of Guizot, Mignet, Thierry and others to press forward the establishment of the *Ecole des Chartes* in 1829 and to publish French historical sources as a sort of counter-blast to the *Monumenta Germaniae Historica*. But their conception of scientific advance took a form unknown to Berlin. The Revolution had brought in its train a systematic rethinking about the nature of society and how modern political structures might be reconstructed. This mood is evident in the writings of Saint-Simon and Louis Blanc. It underpins the astonishing vision of Auguste Comte, whose treatise on positive philosophy (see Comte 1830–42; cf. Standley 1981 and Freund 1992) divided the history of the world into three phases and interpreted everything in terms of what the phases required. None of these writers considered himself an historian. Perhaps Guizot was the first to appropriate these surgical techniques for the writing of history rather than for social prophecy. He saw the corpus of material on which

---

54 The *locus classicus* for this process is Chadwick 1975.

historians worked as literally a corpus – a body – and he certainly had been exposed to the analogy during the Revolution. When he was seven years old in 1794 his father, a Girondin lawyer, went to the guillotine in Nîmes. He fled with his mother to Geneva and spent formative years there, returning home during the Napoleonic period and becoming Professor of Modern History in the *faculté des lettres* in Paris in 1812 where he remained until his retirement in 1849. There he taught that historical science ought to assume the categories of autopsy. One must study anatomy (the collecting of the facts) and physiognomy (the individual features of events) with a view to constructing a physiology (the laws that govern historical events). These formed the tools with which Guizot went to work on the *History of Civilization in France* (1829–32), which the second revolution of 1830 truncated because of his political involvement. The result was arresting all the same and betrayed a commitment to analytical method that marked all his writing and suffused the frequent whispering in the reader's ear about what had to be done.

> I would like to follow in their totality the destinies of feudalism . . . I would not wish to divide it up, but keep it constantly under your eyes, and make you thus see its successive transformations at a single glance. . . . Unfortunately this cannot be. In order to study, the human mind is obliged to divide, to analyse; it only acquires knowledge successively and in pieces. It is then the work of imagination and reason to reconstruct the demolished edifice, to resuscitate the being destroyed by the scientific scalpel. But it is absolutely necessary to pass through this process of dissection . . . [55]

Men closely identified with the fortunes of the new French democracy, such as Guizot and Thiers, articulated one mood. But the next generation had its own tone, perhaps because its background was different but also because it had available and unavoidable the new biblical criticism coming out of Germany in the work of Schleiermacher and Strauss[56] and the climate of extreme scientism engendered by Darwin's discoveries. It appears in one of the century's great teachers whose influence proved more wide-ranging than his writing: Numa

---

55 *Histoire de la civilisation en France*, quoted in Crossley 1993: 84.
56 There is comparatively little in English on David Strauss and Friedrich Schleiermacher. For the former, see Lawler 1986. For Schleiermacher, see Richardson 1991; Forstman 1977.

Denis Fustel de Coulanges. He died before his sixtieth birthday in 1889 but Fustel's command over a generation of young French intellectuals became prodigious. His career as one of the new professionals in the historical field certainly helped him acquire authority. He had been an admirer of Guizot in his youth and had proceeded via the *Ecole Normale* and a teaching position in Amiens to a doctorate on Polybius. But social institutions interested him more than personalities or texts; and having moved to a chair at Strasbourg in 1860 – the year after Darwin's *Origin of Species* appeared – he worked on *La Cité antique*, which, when it was published in 1864, invigorated discussion about religion because it identified the function of religion in the ancient city as one of binding together a given society with the institutions of the state.[57] His removal to the *Ecole Normale* on the strength of his book in 1870 and to a chair at the Sorbonne in 1875 gave him an opportunity radically to remould the opinions of the young.

Gabriel Monod (1844–1912) was not so young: he belonged to the highly talented group who straddled the two centuries and who help explain the shift from an orthodox historiography in France in the mid-nineteenth century to a subversive one after the First World War, as we shall see. Fustel strongly contributed to his education all the same and Monod applied to his own work on the early Franks the same concern with institutions displayed by his teacher (Monod 1895; 1896). More than any other historian working in France in the later nineteenth century, he wanted to drag French thinking into line with German advances in the subject and placed himself at the vortex of a movement to start a major professional journal that could rival the *Historische Zeitschrift*, begun in 1859. The *Revue Historique* owed its foundation in 1876 to Monod's drive. He also took a keen interest in historiography. His *Les Maîtres de l'histoire* (1894) ranks among the first modern studies of other historians. And his choice of subject matter – Michelet, Renan and Taine – has its own suggestiveness.

The force of Renan made itself felt less in historical circles than in theological because his *Vie de Jésus* (1863) caused all the furore in France that David Strauss's *Leben Jesu* had precipitated in Germany in 1835 and Sir John Seeley's *Ecce Homo* was to generate in English

---

57 Fustel de Coulanges 1864. His work is analysed in Hartog 1988.

intellectual circles in 1865. But Taine's determination to alter the nature of historical thinking without his having initially the professional advantages possessed by Fustel or Monod succeeded, at least temporarily, by sheer muscle. Indeed in his case the new 'science' offered the opportunity, seized by a number of nineteenth-century failures, to turn the tables on those who had not seen their genius. Hyppolyte Taine (1828–93) had been a flop at school. He failed his Ph.D. He became a schoolteacher, like Fustel, and then moved to Paris where he became a professional writer with a view about everything. Only in 1865, when he was nearly 40, did the *Ecole des Beaux Arts* offer him a chair in aesthetics; and from there he ruminated about neither aesthetics nor *Beaux Arts* but about the history of France and what had controlled it. *Les Origines de la France contemporaine* (1874–93) did not have three phases as Comte might have wished: it had instead three forces or moments which, between them, explained how history worked.

Few authors capture better than Taine the nightmare of pseudo-science elevated into a philosophy of history. The past became for him literally 'a geometry of forces' (quoted in Chadwick 1975: 205). His analysis of a major event in France's past would look rather like an engineer's drawing that depicts the various moments and thrusts operating on a bridge or a building. Taine would look first, perhaps, at race because his typology of races would suggest a framework within which action took place. He would add in data from the relevant *milieu* (another of his categories) which would provide material to enable him to allow for local peculiarity. Most important of all would then be the *moment* pressing on the event in question; and he defined that, with an impressive imprecision, as the impetus given to the present by the past. In his later years these three forces left Taine with little to laugh about and his correspondence became a review of current degeneration as he saw dogs going for the world out of unstoppable instinct. He insisted to Guizot in 1873:

Science, as soon as she becomes exact, ceases to be revolutionary, becoming even anti-revolutionary. Zoology shows us man's carnivorous teeth; – let us beware of awakening in him his carnivorous and ferocious instincts. Psychology shows us that human reason is based on words and images; – let us beware of provoking in him hallucination, madness. We are told by political economy that there is continual disproportion between population and sustenance; – let us not forget that even in a time of peace and prosperity, the struggle for life is ever going on, and remember not to exacerbate it. History proves to us that the state, government, religion, church, all public institutions, are the only means by which wild and animal man obtains his small share of reason and justice; – let us beware of destroying the flower by cutting at the root.

In short, it appears to me that general science tends towards prudence and conservatism, not towards revolution and for proof of this we need but to study the delicate complexity of the social body.

(Sparvel-Bayly 1908: III, 123–4)

Perhaps it seems harder to think of an English facet to this world of scientific laws and cosmic forces, yet one existed, albeit eccentrically. Henry Thomas Buckle gave ground to no Frenchman in eccentricity: seven miles walked every day, seven hours' reading every day, bread and fruit for lunch every day, master-strength at chess, nineteen languages, 22,000 books, dead by the time he was 41. He lived the life of a gentleman-scholar who had received little academic training but, like Taine, saw this disability as his edge over rival historians. It gave him an overview of several forests where others could only see trees. So in the *History of Civilisation in England* (1857–61), which he never lived to complete, he intended to supply a fresh version of British history by studying systematically what his predecessors had approached randomly and 'accomplish[ing] for the history of man something equivalent, or at all events analogous, to what has been effected by the enquiries for the different branches of natural science'. He needed to wrest the discipline from 'the hands of biographers, genealogists and collectors of anecdotes, chroniclers of courts and princes and nobles, those babblers of vain things'.[58] In practice, he created a deterministic world like Taine's where the explanation for historical events becomes a mechanical exercise in applying the laws of change that Buckle imagined himself to have discovered; and his text reminds a modern reader, as it did de Tocqueville, of what happens when investigations 'end up *at the machine*' (quoted in Semmel 1984: 138). Since religion went the way of everything else in this account, Acton gave the book one of its stormiest reviews. He, too, noted that

---

58 Buckle 1894, 6ff. Antonella Codazzi considers his historiographical significance and relation to Taine in *Hyppolyte Taine e il progetto filosofico di una storiografia scientifica* (1985).

Buckle 'look[ed] at men not as persons, but as machines' which enabled him to agglomerate them into bogus collectivities:

> The true historian takes the individual for his centre. . . . If he treats of mobs, or armies, or bodies of men, he invests this multitude with a kind of personality of its own – its own wishes, passions, character, will, and conscience. Mr. Buckle's history, if he *could* write a history according to this programme, would be the reverse of all this: he would merge the individual in the company, the person in the body, wishes, passions, character, conscience, all would be abstracted. . . . History would consist in tabular views of births, deaths, marriages, diseases, prices, commerce and the like; and the historian would be chiefly useful in providing grocers with cheap paper to wrap up butter in.
>
> (quoted in McNeill 1967: 17)

It was magnificently unfair and not a little prescient.

Nevertheless, the impact of scientific aspiration if not of execution could not be gainsaid, except by those such as Herbert Spencer who could gain by saying it. His allegation that historians were not only incapable themselves of developing social science but guilty of denying its possibility when others attempted it (Spencer 1904: II, 253) has more to do with his vainglory than what historians thought and wrote. Politically correct critics such as Henry Sidgwick disapproved of the violence which Buckle had met in the reviews. 'Abuse him as you like,' he wrote to a friend, 'he is the first Englishman who has attempted to write scientific history.'[59] A book like Walter Bagehot's *Physics and Politics* (1872) said volumes in its title about this gathering mood[60] and by 1875 the economist (and historian) J. E. Cairnes had reached conclusions quite different from Spencer's about the acceptance of science:

> There is a certain sense in which, I presume, the doctrine of 'Social Evolution' would be now pretty widely accepted, at least among those who have concerned themselves with the philosophy of history and kindred speculations. I mean the sense in which it expresses the fact that each stage in human progress is the outcome and result of the stage which has immediately preceded it, and that the whole series of stages . . . represents a connected chain, of which the links are bound together as sequences in

---

59 Sidgwick to Dakyns, 24 Aug. 1861, in Sidgwick and Sidgwick 1906: 68.
60 It also reflected expressly on history which '[e]very one now admits . . . is guided by certain laws': Bagehot 1872: 42.

precisely the same way as in the instances of causation presented by other departments of nature. Some such assumption as this must necessarily form the basis of all attempts at a rational interpretation of history.

(Cairnes 1875: 64)

That such support should come from an economist reminds us of one crucial area of 'scientific' history that responded especially well to the climate of the late nineteenth century. Germany perhaps began the swing towards economic history, not least because of her own industrial revolution and the presence of a Marxist understanding of economic processes, and the story was taken up strongly in Britain where classical 'political economy' had fallen prey by the 1870s to the mathematical models of Stanley Jevons and the revolution in economic ideas spearheaded in Cambridge. The economic history pioneered by W. J. Ashley and William Cunningham[61] began an important national tradition that would mature only after the Second World War. In Germany the 'national' economic history revolving around Hildebrand, originally, and then Roscher, Knies and Schmoller[62] continued the project of dissection, rejecting economic theory with its cardboard models of human practice and insisting on the need for substantive accounts of real processes – on the need, in other words, for historical method. Here explanation took its power from actuality and history took its shape from experience revealed in detailed historical research. Problems would appear at the point, evident by the

---

61 William Cunningham (1849–1919) can be approached through Audrey Cunningham, *William Cunningham, Teacher and Priest* (1950). Among the more important of his books one might count *The Growth of English Industry and Commerce* (1882) and *Modern Civilisation in Some of its Economic Aspects* (1896). W. J. (later Sir William) Ashley (1860–1927) was impressively prolific across a chronological range that would overwhelm most modern scholars. The most seminal of the larger studies was *An Introduction to English Economic History and Theory* (1888–93).

62 The phenomenon as a whole is considered in Winkel 1977 and Krüger 1983. Bruno Hildebrand (d. 1878) had founded the *Jahrbücher für Nationalökonomie und Statistik* but Carl Knies and Wilhelm Roscher recommended the specifically historical treatment of the subject in their respective works, perhaps most significantly in Knies's *Die politischen Oekonomie vom Standpunkte der geschichtlichen Methode* (2nd edn, 1883). Gustav Schmoller carried these perceptions into a variety of social and political studies, as well as one major historical work, *Umrisse und Untersuchungen zur Verfassungs- Verwaltungs- und Wirtschaftsgeschichte besonders des preussischen Staates im 17. und 18. Jahrhundert* (1898).

1880s, when economics wished to take leave of 'political economy' and become its own science.

The sheer definitiveness of dealing in hard data caught the imagination of historians overpowered by the loss of familiar reference-points or tormented by the *Methodenstreit* in Germany, which we shall examine shortly. But of course the need to clarify social action by analysis and comparison would not stop there, especially when the late nineteenth century had seen the spawning of new intellectual fields of enquiry such as sociology, psychology and anthropology. If the second half of the century was the apogee of Marx, then it was also the epoch of Frazer and Tylor, of Croce and Dilthey, of Emile Durkheim and Gustave Le Bon. It combats credibility to see all historians of the period immolated behind an unthinking empiricism, even if many of them continued to see themselves in the tradition of a Rankean objectivity, looking for more facts to unearth. If there were an example of that myopia, perhaps America might best suggest it. Certainly John Higham was less than generous about the American commitment to 'science'. 'Scientific history tended towards a rigid factualism every-where in the late nineteenth century,' he wrote,

> but perhaps nowhere more strongly than among American professionals. Unlike their contemporary colleagues in England, France and Germany, the Americans made not a single sustained effort to discuss the nature of historical knowledge. Even in the handbooks they wrote on historical method, American scholars dispensed with the theoretical sections of the European treatises – chiefly Ernst Bernheim's *Lehrbuch der historischen Methode* (1889) – on which they otherwise relied.
>
> (Higham *et al.* 1965)

In this sense the scientific spirit of enquiry might lead in directions which no apostle of 'processes' and 'phases' had the imagination to conceive. The early work of Wilhelm Dilthey had concerned itself with psychological investigation: he changed to thinking about history only when he decided that history was the true psychology. The disreputable young scholar of Leipzig, Karl Lamprecht, likewise found his scientific inclinations taking him further down the road of a comparative history that would interest itself not with quantifiable data generated by past societies, but with their *Weltanschauungen*, for the analysis of which historians would need to master more than one discipline. Working on a journal called the *Archiv für Kulturgeschichte*, he became ever more deeply involved in a new element in historical enquiry that would lead him and his generation towards a further broadening of the subject. But there was nothing inevitable about that turn. Nor was it clear that historians ought to take it.

6

CULTURE AND *KULTUR*

The need for a history of 'culture' sprang from deep roots in German historical consciousness. Lamprecht's journal of 1894 merely retitled an existing one, the *Zeitschrift für deutsche Kulturgeschichte*, which two men in particular, Johannes Falke and Johann Müller, had helped inaugurate as early as 1856. (Gilbert 1990: 84). An insistence on the Germanic character of *Kultur* followed predictably enough from the search for origins which we have noticed in the generation of Humboldt and the young Ranke; and its meaning proved limited in practice to a form of social history that tried to press exploration beyond the elites on whom historians normally concentrated. By the time Karl Lamprecht went up to Göttingen as an undergraduate in 1874, however, the connotations of a cultural history had begun the series of shifts which would eventually make two distinct patterns discernible. One of them reflected an interest in a new historical form arising from the history of art and literature as keys to understanding social perception and the limits of a period's sense of itself. This tendency prowled around the edge of the German Empire in Switzerland, Belgium and Holland. The other predilection saw in *Kultur* a concept that associated intellectual and aesthetic prowess with a definite understanding of state–ascendancy and tied its analysis of German thought to the development of the Bismarckian Reich. Even Lamprecht, who dissociated himself from some aspects of this reduction of *Kultur* to *Macht*, found himself amid the dislocations of 1914 looking back on what he saw as an 'extraordinarily strong distinction between west European cultural formation [*Kulturverhalten*] and the central European, especially German, one'; and he saw in the latter's peculiarity 'a close connection between state and nation' (Lamprecht 1914: 9, 11).

Few inhabitants of continental Europe were to escape that peculiarity between 1870 and 1914, and the rationale adopted by Berlin for German policy had an explicit cultural content. When Western cartoons satirizing the German army appeared during the First World War, a favourite theme lay, therefore, in depicting babies skewered on German bayonets over a caption exclaiming 'Another Example of German *Kultur*!' Nor was it accidental that the celebration among European historians of high culture as a resistance against the evils inherent in mass industrialized society reached its apogee among those at once close to the German *Kulturnation* yet nervous of its potential for harm. Lamprecht's journey, from a notion of culture to a modified acceptance of *Kultur* as his nation went off to war with full and pure hearts in search of a rich future,[63] symbolized one way in which these categories elided. An alternative itinerary, one infinitely more significant for the future of cultural historiography, started in Basle, went to Berlin and came back again.

Quite what to make of the writings of Jacob Burckhardt (1818–97) poses more problems today than it might have done fifty years ago. The recluse who refused Ranke's chair to live alone above a baker's shop in his home town seems attractive to the modern understanding of what an intellectual ought to be. Conversely, his anti-Semitism, loathing for the masses and cultural pessimism does not endear him to modern liberals.[64] Most of these worries turn on Burckhardt's later work and one readily forgets just how much he had swallowed *Kultur* as a young student in Ranke's Berlin. 'I have Germany to thank for everything!', an early letter reported. 'What a people! What a wonderful youth! What a land – a paradise!'[65] But the revolution had dismayed him in 1848:

---

63 'Unsere Herzen waren rein und waren gross, und sie waren voll des Gedankens an eine reiche Zukunft unserer Nation' (Lamprecht 1914: 15).
64 Even so gifted a critic as Hayden White has a mild fit of modernity when presenting Burckhardt's world-view and his essay does not have the conviction of those on Ranke and Michelet. Cf. White 1973: 230–64.
65 Quoted in Hugh Trevor-Roper's introduction to Jacob Burckhardt, *On History and Historians* (1965), xiii. Cf. Trevor-Roper 1984.

The word freedom sounds rich and beautiful, but no one should talk about it who has not seen and experienced slavery under the loud-mouthed masses, called 'the people', seen it with his own eyes and endured civil unrest . . . I know too much about history to expect anything from the despotism of the masses but a future tyranny, which will mean the end of history.

(quoted in White 1973: 235)

In returning to Switzerland, he largely turned his back on the German dream and immersed himself in Renaissance art and literature, perhaps looking for that 'intoxication' or 'consolation' which Croce (1941: 104–5, 107) saw at the heart of Burckhardt's historical thought. Whatever his motivation, the book that ultimately resulted – *The Civilization of the Renaissance in Italy (Die Kultur der Renaissance in Italien)* – would come to have an importance quite overlooked at the time of its publication in 1860.

It was not his first book. Contact with Droysen in Berlin and Gottfried Kinkel at Bonn had taken his mind towards classical Greece and he had later written both a life of Constantine and *Cicerone* (1855), a guide to Italian painting. The rediscovery of that world in the Renaissance marked the awakening of spirit that he sought and missed in the Germany he had come to know; and it offered an opportunity to write about the state in a new way. Not that political history takes up much of his time: it is dispatched in a first chapter which shows the preconditions in state development that would allow the Italian Renaissance to happen. But the *Leitmotif* of those changes – the emergence of the 'individual' – he sees as both an ingredient in cultural arousal and a matter for personal celebration. Before the reader's eyes Burckhardt then exposes a series of what he calls 'cross-sections' dealing with aspects of the Renaissance environment: the revival of antiquity, the discovery of the world and its encapsulation in a new literature concerned with 'the daily course of human life':

> The comical and satirical literature of the Middle Ages could not dispense with pictures of every-day events. But it was another thing, when the Italians of the Renaissance dwelt on this picture for its own sake – for its inherent interest – and because it forms part of that great, universal life of the world whose magic breath they felt everywhere around them. Instead of and together with the satirical comedy, which wanders through houses, villages and streets, seeking food for its derision in parson, peasant and burgher, we now see in literature the beginnings of a true *genre*, long before it found any expression in painting.

(Burckhardt n.d.: 181)

From here he heads towards society and festivals, morality and religion. Not only did such a structure mark a new departure in content, moreover, but it also has claims to constitute the first attempt in Western historiography to write a book in a non-narrative way. For although it makes use of chronology within its various sections to organize the presentation of argument, the book as whole lacks a chronological origin and terminus. *Die Kultur der Renaissance in Italien* made use, moreover, of categories of material that never before had been systematically deployed for a historical, rather than aesthetic, purpose – especially the visual arts and poetry, 'one of history's most important, singular [*allereinste*] and beautiful sources' (Burckhardt [1905] 1955: 69).

In the short term, Burckhardt's conspectus won little acclaim. Ruskin knew about him in England; perhaps Acton also helped to promote his name there (Kaegi 1962: 81). It was rather towards the end of the century, when current moods about decadence in Western civilization helped stimulate interest in cultural literature, that the book began to acquire a readership and Burckhardt his first disciples. It must have been in the early years of the twentieth century that a Dutch schoolboy or young student, Johan Huizinga, first read him and became persuaded of the need for a new form of historical statement.[66] But by then of course the world had changed radically and Burckhardt's *Weltgeschichtliche Betrachtungen* (1905) showed that he had changed too. He had been offended by the willingness of German apostles of *Kultur* to receive Darwinist teaching into their definition of cultural development; and the Bismarckian invasion of France in 1870 left him profoundly disturbed. In the Europe of the second industrial revolution he was left lamenting that everything would soon '*business* werden wie in Amerika'.[67] He became to historiography what Nietzsche had become to Germanic philosophy: the achievement lost itself in a clutch of catch-phrases. His later work shows a closer approximation, in fact, to the drift of his generation in seeing the state as a critical element in explanation and places *language*,

---

66 Huizinga's intellectual debts are traced in Collie 1964.
67 Reflection dated March 1873 in Burckhardt [1905] 1955: 203 (emphasis added).

rather than art or high culture, at the centre of the picture, together with race and blood.[68]

Race and blood had meanwhile darkened their stain in Lamprecht's Germany. In the year he went to Göttingen, Heinrich von Treitschke (1834–96) succeeded Ranke in the Berlin chair, having already moved away from his earlier liberalism to a state-led conception of society reflected in his history of Germany (Treitschke 1879–94). His pupil Friedrich Meinecke (1862–1954) helped Treitschke become chief editor of the prestigious *Historische Zeitschrift* on the death of Sybel in 1895; and when Treitschke himself died in the following year, Meinecke took over and held the position until the Nazis deposed him in 1935. In all these writers, as with Gustav Droysen and Ernst Troeltsch, the mood of Wilhelmine Germany infected their histories with a sense of Prussian triumphalism and a rethinking of the basis of ethics away from individual volition and towards the state as its own 'ethical unit of will'.[69] The idea of a *Kulturnation* had begun its trajectory towards a *Staatsnation* or, worse, the one had become subsumed in the other. Now Lamprecht, established since 1891 in a chair at Leipzig which he was to hold until his death in 1915, reacted archly against all forms of mysticism, whether in the form of Kantian Idealism or Treitschkian elegiacs about the Fatherland. His own *Deutsche Geschichte*, which began to appear from 1891, implied a different perspective. To be sure, Lamprecht felt a commitment to German *Kultur*. But his historical method had more to do with the comparative analysis of various kinds of culture than with the promotion of a particular one. He accepted that the state must lie at the centre of the analysis but taught that the Rankians had erred in missing the degree to which broad cultural forces determine outcomes rather than localized intentions. As a pupil of Roscher, he understood economies to play a salient role, as his early book on German economic life in the Middle Ages attested (Lamprecht 1885–6). And the enormous project he conceived on the history of German culture, for all its dwelling on

---

68 Ibid. 57–8. He saw culture finally as one of three 'Potenzen' in the world; religion and the state formed the other two. But he retained a commitment to 'die Gesellschaft im weitersten Sinne'.

69 Ernst Troeltsch, quoted in Iggers 1983: 186.

political narrative, would come to manifest a commitment to a moral undertow in the narrative, as his biographer explains:

> Lamprecht did not define this concept [of culture] in the *German History* ... but his account made it clear that culture was foremost an ethical matter. It related to the regulation of behavior. Cultural progress meant the transition from collective to individual constraint, from external compulsion to internal discipline and freedom. Primitive civilizations were 'ruled by dark drives,' which were bridled by the collective compulsion exerted by family, clan and tribe. The development of culture then passed, in Lamprecht's analysis, through stages characterized successively by the appearance of legal order, the discipline of social convention, and the emergence of a sense of individual moral duty. It was no coincidence that culture developed through the same stages, marked out by the same historical periods, as did national consciousness, for the two were ultimately the same[70]

In all of this, most of all in his decision to establish a chronology in accordance with supposed aesthetic and symbolic transformations, he recalls Burckhardt, whom we know him to have studied. But the Treitschkian side also remained with him. He recognized that different states would produce different cultural formations with a scientific value of their own. That is why he commissioned Henri Pirenne to write a history of Belgium for his series on the history of European states.[71]

The two men had corresponded since 1894 and one of the sadnesses of increasing chauvinism in the twentieth century lay in its disruption of their relationship. Without having known Lamprecht, on the other hand, Pirenne would in any case have acquired a clear grasp of methodological trends in Germany where he spent a year after his graduation from Liège. He also worked with Monod and Fustel in Paris for a year: fulfilling the logic of his country's history so that he became neither French nor German. His own contribution to the idea of cultural history did not, like Lamprecht's, have the state at its core. Neither did it turn on an aesthetic perception, as Burckhardt's had done. Pirenne's historical writing had affinities with an earlier understanding of culture

---

70 Chickering 1993: 136. I draw on this important study at a number of points in my account.

71 The background to the *Europäische Staatengeschichte* is presented in Chickering 1993: 166. Lamprecht outlined his own approach in his *Die Kulturhistorische Methode* (1900).

as the presentation of a global social and economic account. In his hands, however, it would become so much more than that.

Belgium itself – its geography, its linguistic and cultural blend – does something to explain the thrust of Pirenne's interests and career. In the late nineteenth century Belgian intellectual life had discovered a new self-confidence, especially in the University of Liège where Emile de Laveleye (1822–92) taught economics but also established a reputation in the higher journalism of western Europe, including England, for his contribution to the 'socialism of the chair'. He strongly influenced a young colleague, Paul Frédéricq, who taught in Liège for a few years before moving back to his home environment at Ghent where he had completed his doctorate. Frédéricq's passion was for *teaching*: he studied it as others researched their sources. While teaching at Liège, he began his expeditions to other universities in Germany and England to discover how they taught history; and his conclusions appeared in a book about *Better Teaching in History* at the turn of the century (Frédéricq 1899). As a working historian, he developed an expertise on the Spanish Inquisition in the Low Countries.[72] All of this impinged greatly on Pirenne because he took three courses with Frédéricq as an undergraduate. Like Frédéricq, moreover, Pirenne wanted to travel. His two years spent in Germany and France gave him a sharp sense of how historical work might be approached from radically divergent directions. His own studies often display the stronger qualities of each.

Pirenne's period was the early Middle Ages, his territory the Pays-Bas. But his definition of both defied convention. If his name is now associated particularly with the economic and social structures of northern Europe and the towns and institutions that arose there, it is typical of him that he should have seen the rise of Islam as contributing centrally to the creation of his subject matter.[73] Similarly, the Pays-Bas connoted for him a tract of territory stretching from northern France, through Flanders and into modern Holland. Even so wide a

---

72 For information on Frédéricq, see Lyon, 1974: 40ff.

73 The so-called 'Pirenne thesis' identified the rise of Islam in the seventh century as the cataclysm which disrupted the economic life of southern Europe and turned the northern periphery into the centre of a new Carolingian civilization. For a recent re-evaluation see Hodges and Whitehouse 1983.

perspective, moreover, never occludes Pirenne's assumption that he is speaking about 'l'Europe occidentale' against which all subsets of information must be gauged. Within those categories he concerned himself more with the interaction of geography and social formations than with administrative boundaries and political questions. The exception that proved the rule happened to be his masterpiece, the *Histoire de Belgique*, but there the constraints of Lamprecht and his fellow editors sometimes feel fairly strong. The idea of depicting Belgium as a cohesive culture that thrived on internal difference rather than suffering atrophy from it was the central perception that only a mind like Pirenne's would have seen. Having announced it, he proceeds in fairly conventional terms; he spends time on literature and art – more than would be usual at the time he wrote – but the political account leads strongly once he is out of his own period and presumably relying on secondary sources that have a mostly political orientation.

In his own period Pirenne studied cultures in the way a biologist does: under the microscope. But because he believed that results can be applied across territories, his work always had an implicit commitment to *comparative* study. Here is an example from a page in *Les Anciennes Démocraties des Pays-Bas* which appeared in 1910. The French is retained to illustrate Pirenne's economy and simplicity, which often verges on the terse:

> En France et en Angleterre, le pouvoir royal fut assez puissant pour s'opposer tout d'abord aux tentatives urbaines, puis pour en triompher. En Italie et en Allemagne, sa faiblesse le condamna au contraire à capituler devant elles, et une riche floraison de villes libres s'épanouit bientôt des deux côtés des Alpes. Quant aux Pays-Bas, ils présentent une situation intermédiaire . . . [Ses grandes communes] diffèrent tout à la fois des *freie Reichstädte* de l'Empire ou des républiques municipales de la Toscone et des communes de France étroitement surveillées par les prévôts and les baillis du roi.
>
> (Pirenne 1910)

Pirenne's own story runs through into the 1930s and his unfinished *Muhammad and Charlemagne*. But long before 1914 he had contributed enough to show how the history of a national or regional culture might be attempted and he had done so in face of an *étatisme* which had begun to turn Europe into an armed camp.

Burckhardt never saw much of that except in his mind's eye; he died in 1897. Pirenne would see too much of it in his internment camp in Germany during the First World War. Culture as an ambition had not died, but then neither had *Kultur*: an unknown schoolteacher in Wilhelmine Germany had already committed himself to saving the latter, if only to follow the logic of History as its great wheel turned once more to crush the declining 'civilization' of the West (Spengler [1918–23] 1926–9). The two senses of cultural history came together more poignantly in the life of another schoolteacher who became a professional academic and eventually Holland's greatest historian of the twentieth century. For Huizinga maintained much of the Burckhardtian legacy, looking for his material in poetry, encapsulating the *Geist* of an entire period, seeing no difficulty in discussing *The Waning of the Middle Ages* as though an epoch could lose its sense of itself (Huizinga [1919] 1924). Culture continued in his hands to mean intellectual and aesthetic cultivation; and social elites were necessary for sustaining it. Like Toynbee, he saw barbarism as the natural ally of democracy. Like Burckhardt, he avoided the dwelling on materialism that he saw as characteristic of his day by transporting himself to more propitious periods in his private imagination. In 1940 his country felt the force of *Kultur*: the experience of Huizinga re-ran the narrative of Pirenne in 1915 with the patriotic self-closure of his university and his internment at the hands of the invading Germans. He was not taken to a field and shot, like Marc Bloch; he died along with thousands of his countrymen in the ravaging Dutch winter of 1944–5 when no food could be found. So there was an acrid irony. He was killed by the very element that his history had always excluded. 'Culture' in his sense survived him in the history of art and music, but as a force in historical research it underwent a definitional (and generational) transformation. *Kultur* became an embarrassment or a capitalist symptom. The next thirty years would bring cultural history to a new height of popularity and influence only when it turned itself into an intellectual form that neither Meinecke nor Huizinga would have appreciated.

7

THE ENGLISH 'WHIGS'

At first sight, the British avoided the rise of cultural history. The symptoms of an historiographical mood which they shared in the Romantic period with France and Germany and America seem to have disappeared thereafter. Of course, there remained 'influences'. Ranke became a model for many historians who were engaged in serious work and held his popularity until the German Empire began its change of direction towards an assertive imperialism after 1871 and lost its veneration for British practice.[74] The more cosmopolitan historians in Britain, with Acton at their head, read widely in French and German and presumably sensed changes afoot on the Continent. For the most part, however, Britain, like the United States, went its own way. The result was a distinctive and remarkably time-specific tendency which focused on British experience at the expense of the world outside, one that concentrated on types of constitutional history rather than on social, cultural or intellectual studies, and that often imbued that study with linear logic leading from past to present, so that history became a matter of identifying broad processes working themselves out over hundreds of years and connecting the present of Victorian Westminster with a past running back through the Glorious

---

74 For this development see McClelland 1971; cf Sheehan 1978.

Revolution, Magna Carta, the Witanagemot and eventually towards the forests of Saxony. The doctrines associated with this history were congratulatory: the story celebrated English (as opposed, mostly, to Scottish, Welsh or Irish) liberty and the institutions that it deemed central to the widening of English freedom through the ages. And they were *colligatory*.[75] Events across long spans of time could be sewn together in a common story of success as though the historian's thread were as strong and endless as his tapestry. For Edward Freeman (1823–92) William the Conqueror and William III who 'delivered' England in the Revolution of 1689 attracted comparison as though the 600 years between them only heightened their mutual relation.

> In the one case the invader came to conquer, in the other he came to deliver; but in both cases alike the effect of his coming was to preserve and not to destroy; the Conqueror and the Deliverer alike has had his share in working out the continuous being of English law and of English national life . . . [B]oth revolutions have worked for the same end; the great actors in both were, however unwittingly, fellow-workers in the same cause.[76]

In 1931 Herbert Butterfield published a typology of such approaches under the title *The Whig Interpretation of History* which gained a great vogue during the next two or three decades and fixed the nineteenth century, to its detriment, with a ready-made critique which lesser historians than Butterfield have applied mechanically to several generations of writers. Butterfield's short meditation – it was hardly more than an essay – singled out no particular men for attack; it offered no index. It took its starting-point from discomfort in the face of writers (and here he plainly had Acton in mind) who used historical work as a way of executing judgement on the past and exacting vengeance on malefactors. Instead, 'research' had a different task. It should illuminate

---

75 A very useful term reinvented by W. H. Walsh from its origin in the nineteenth-century Cambridge mathematician and philosopher, Whewell. See Walsh [1951] 1992: 23–4. Colligation is the activity of binding together a narrative (and thus rescuing it from mere sequence) by deciding how events in a given story can be made to tie in with one another. A permanent problem for philosophers of history lies in establishing whether colligation is something that historians achieve despite the incoherence of their subject matter or whether colligation is already inherent in the world that they merely describe and report. For divergent readings of this difficulty, cf. Carr 1986 and White 1987.
76 Quoted in Burrow 1981: 196. This section draws heavily on Professor Burrow's work.

the past as it appeared to those for whom it was the present, rather than treating historical persons as though they were apprentice-figures, trying and often failing to be modern:

> Real historical understanding is not achieved by the subordination of the past to the present, but rather by our making the past our present and attempting to see life with the eyes of another century than our own. It is not reached by assuming that our own age is the absolute to which Luther and Calvin and their generation are only relative; it is only reached by fully accepting the fact that their generation was as valid as our generation, their issues as momentous as our issues and their day as full and vital to them as our day is to us.

> (Butterfield [1931] 1973: 20–1)

This says little more than Ranke had said. Where Butterfield went further was in his perception that bad history functioned by abridgement: it simplified a complex story and bent its inner linkages by leaving out all those facts that got in the way of the moral:

> for both the method and the kind of history that results from it would be impossible if all the facts were told in all their fullness. The theory that is behind the whig interpretation – the theory that we study the past for the sake of the present – is one that is really introduced for the purpose of facilitating the abridgement of history; and its effect is to provide us with a handy rule of thumb by which we can easily discover what was important in the past. . . . No one could mistake the aptness of this theory for a school of writers who might show the least inclination to undervalue one side of the historical story; and indeed there would be no point in holding it if it were not for the fact that it serves to simplify the study of history by providing an excuse for leaving things out.

> (ibid. 25–6)

Leaving aside the problems raised by Butterfield's own implied views about selection in history, a difficulty has emerged from labelling as 'Whigs' his disliked historians. Since Whigs appear in British and not European political history, his doctrines have come to be seen as a commentary on a school of British historians, though not, oddly, on American ones where the term 'Whig' also came into prominence during the Reconstruction period. They are held to have their origin in the reaction against Hume's 'Tory' version of the seventeenth century in Hallam and Macaulay and to persist as a tradition in historical writing until at least the high period of George Macaulay Trevelyan in the 1920s and 1930s. Between those terminal dates a canon of historians comprising, among others, William Stubbs, James Anthony Froude,

E. A. Freeman, J. R. Green, W. E. H. Lecky, Lord Acton, J. R. Seeley, S. R. Gardiner, C. H. Firth and J. B. Bury come into focus all too often as embodiments of 'Whig' attitudes with no sense of what made them different from one another or any idea of how the nineteenth century changed in its assumptions. But then, that is what the Whig theory has done: it provides insight into 100 years of historiography by telling posterity what all historians had in common rather than establishing criteria that might help differentiate them. That commonality, moreover, reached far beyond those who could be held guilty of 'Whig' attitudes. Indeed the only nineteenth-century British historian who was not a Whig, on Butterfield's understanding, was Carlyle, unless one extends the title of historian to the Tory firebrand Sir Archibald Alison.[77] Recent writing has proved more astringent and it seems possible both to separate out chronological phases in nineteenth-century writing and to see the role of religion within them as an important determinant of attitude.

Religion remained central to the intellectual environment in Britain during the nineteenth century in a way and to a degree that continental experience did not replicate. Britain did not possess, to be sure, the confessional complications of Belgium and France; nor did the established Church retain that mastery over secular institutions that the Roman Catholic Church continued to enjoy in Spain and Italy. But the insecurities and the questions that gave rise to them invigorated religion as an intellectual domain and contributed in a major fashion to historical understanding. Carlyle apart, the so-called Whigs were predominantly Christian, predominantly Anglican, thinkers for whom the Reformation supplied the critical theatre of enquiry when considering the origins of modern England. When they wrote about the history of the English constitution, as so many of them did, they approached their story from the standpoint of having Good News to relate. Sometimes (since some of these authors were bishops or ordained priests) their commentary edged over into direct homily. More often it

---

77 Sir Archibald Alison (1792–1867) wrote many vast books informed by invincible Toryism. The best-known and most vast are the *History of Europe during the French Revolution* (1833–42) and the *History of Europe from the Fall of Napoleon in 1815 to the Accession of Louis Napoleon in 1852* (1853–9). He reflected on his achievements in *Some Account of my Life and Writings: an Autobiography* (1883).

took the form of eternal breeziness, thankfulness and oblique reference to universal truth.[78] They registered their gratitude for the British way of life, following the example of Freeman who, as John Burrow acutely observes, spoke of his medieval people and institutions like 'a proud or anxious relative'. (Burrow 1981: 199). They wrote, too, in an age innocent of tragedy on the scale known to the century that followed. If they could not have found the grandeur that they developed had they been writing half a century earlier, neither could they have supported their optimism had they lived to endure the barbarisms of the Somme and Passchendaele. In a remarkably stark fashion, the tone of English constitutional history in the second half of the nineteenth century spoke to a specific condition of place and time.

The year 1849 marks a point of origin because in that year appeared John Mitchell Kemble's account of the Saxons and their role, as he conceived it, in the foundation of British political institutions (Kemble 1849). His work reflected the *völkisch* mood of the Germans (he had spent time working with Jakob Grimm) but it also signalled the end of a willingness to see Magna Carta as *fons et origo* for British constitutional development. Macaulay and his contemporaries pressed backward Hume's concern with the seventeenth century to the events of the thirteenth century in their search for the beginning of modernity: Runnymede in 1215, the baronial wars in 1258–65, the calling of the knights to Parliament in 1295. They had begun to outgrow Hume's characterization of the pre-Norman period which is delicious enough to stand recollection:

> With regard to the manners of the Anglo-Saxons we can say little, but that they were in general a rude, uncultivated people, ignorant of letters, unskilled in the mechanical arts, untamed to submission under law and government, addicted to intemperance, riot and disorder. . . . Even the Norman historians, notwithstanding the low state of the arts in their own country, speak of them as barbarians.
>
> (Hume 1754–62: I, 305–6)

But despite the efforts of Sharon Turner (1768–1847)[79] and

---

78 I have commented on their proclivities elsewhere: see Bentley 1993.
79 Principally a philologist, he had studied Icelandic and Anglo-Saxon. The four volumes of his *History of England from the Earliest Period to the Norman Conquest* (1799–1805) drew for the first time on manuscripts in the Cotton Collection.

Benjamin Thorpe (1782–1870)[80] the Anglo–Saxon period retained its image of bone-gnawing savagery until Kemble advanced the suggestion of a fundamental continuity between the world of the Saxons and that of the Norman kingdom that followed. Kemble disliked the Saxons on a number of grounds but a recent scholar sees him as having given 'very balanced accounts of the Roman contribution to the conversion of the Saxons, of the influence of Canon Law, and of the previously notorious career of St. Dunstan' (Smith 1987: 199). Yet what might be termed a 'continuity thesis' received its strongest support from Edward Augustus Freeman (1823–92) in his account of the Norman conquest (Freeman 1867–9), which, together with the more generous appreciation of the relationship between Saxon and Norman England in his *Select Charters* of 1860, marks a high point in mid-Victorian constitutionalism. Between them, Stubbs, Freeman and John Richard Green (1837–83), whose *Short History of the English People* (1874) may be added to the litany, helped establish a climate of composition in which British history assumed a particular shape: 'England' emerged from the Teutonic migrants from northern Germany; it was confirmed in the events of the Norman invasion, sullied by the Angevins, rescued by the barons. Then, Maitland said in recalling Stubbs,

> [s]omewhere about the year 1307 the strain of the triumphal march must be abandoned; we pass in those well-known words 'from the age of heroism to the age of chivalry, from a century ennobled by devotion and self-sacrifice to one in which the gloss of superficial refinement fails to hide the reality of heartless selfishness and moral degradation'.
>
> (Maitland [1901] 1957: 272–3)

The way was open for the factious wars of the fifteenth century, the Tudor Tyranny and the rescue-bid of William III. Stubbs was too discerning a historian and too considerable a Tory to swallow much of this prospectus; but in Freeman's hands it became a hallowed story of aspiring and inspiring liberty within which William the Conqueror and William the Deliverer became equally Gladstonian in their consequences.

---

80 Thorpe, like Kemble, had studied abroad. He spent four years in Copenhagen working with R. C. Rask. His central text on the Anglo–Saxon period is *Ancient Laws and Institutes of England* (1840).

Hallam and Macaulay had commented on some facets of this picture in the 1820s and 1830s. But the generation of Stubbs and Freeman hated the rhetoric and lack of documentation which they associated with the romantics and loaded their accounts with evidence from primary sources. Because James Anthony Froude did that, too, his work provided constitutional historians with an unsavoury problem. His *magnum opus* covered a period of the sixteenth century that touched the nerves of Protestantism and provided a key element in the history of repression (Froude 1856–70). Froude's account made no attempt to camouflage his defence of the Reformation; nor did he mitigate his almost pathological defence of Henry VIII. He used new primary material, moreover, to strike out on his new path and (according to critics) mistranscribed and corrupted it.[81] Between Froude and Freeman, therefore, the journals rang with abuse and counter-claim as the volumes proceeded. Only with Freeman's own excoriation at the hands of John Horace Round in the 1890s did the dismissal of Froude's writing lessen in its severity. Far more acceptable to historical opinion was the mammoth research project of S. R. Gardiner (1829–1902), whose sixteen volumes (Gardiner 1883–4; 1886–91; 1894–1901) on the constitutional history of the seventeenth century (eighteen if one counts the continuation by Stubbs's pupil, Charles Harding Firth)[82] lent renewed force to the idea of a Puritan revolution having marked an outbreak of liberation against the forces of darkness.

But of course figures other than Froude posed a challenge to 'Whig' notions of constitutional change by the turn of century. Those notions' essential connectedness and vaunted continuities suffered from Round, who destroyed key items of Freeman's understanding of the Norman Conquest in a series of articles beginning in 1891 and collected in his *Feudal England* (1895), and Frederic William Maitland whose enquiries into the bases of English law rendered untenable the

---

81 Much of the criticism of Froude seems small-minded in retrospect when one considers his assiduity in researching archives in Spain and his determination to write history from authentic primary material. His mistakes have not been found to compromise his argument (though many other weaknesses have done so) and although his history was infected with doctrines that he did not pretend to hide, so were the thoughts of his critics. 82 *The Last Years of the Protectorate 1656–58* (2 vols, 1909) was a self-conscious extension and one 'undertaken with Dr Gardiner's wishes' (ibid. 5).

Stubbsian analysis of, in particular, the nature and status of the English Parliament at the beginning of the fourteenth century.[83] In the later part of the chronology, meanwhile, J. R. Seeley's teaching on the nature of the state and the degree to which its growth must be sought in external considerations rather than some internally generated efflorescence did little to help the model provided in the 1860s and 1870s (see Seeley 1883 and 1895). Even Froude's dyspeptic defence of the sixteenth century came to have a more sophisticated champion in the work of A. F. Pollard (1869–1948), who was later to found London's Institute of Historical Research.[84] Indeed the faithful themselves had come by the turn of the century to reflect on how different 'Whig' history had become since the time of Macaulay:

> [T]he politics of the seventeenth century, when studied for the mere sake of understanding them, assume a very different appearance from that which they had in the eyes of men who, like Macaulay and Forster,[85] regarded them through the medium of their own political struggles. Eliot and Strafford were neither Whigs nor Tories, Liberals nor Conservatives. As Professor Seeley was, I believe, the first to teach directly, though the lesson is indirectly involved in every line written by Ranke ... the constant or unavowed comparison of [the past] with the present ... is altogether destructive of real historical knowledge.
>
> (Gardiner 1883–4: I, vi)

Far from presenting a constant picture of advance towards Protestant liberty, British history had come to have a more complicated aspect by 1900. Why, though, did the complication leave British historiography still looking very different from that in the rest of Europe? Why, with the partial exception of Green, did it produce no social historian? Why no English Burckhardt or Pirenne?

---

83 Maitland's beautifully constructed critique, which devastates through its relentless civility, forms the introduction to his edition of the *Records of the Parliament holden at Westminster, on the 28th day of February, 1305* (Rolls Series, 1893) reprinted in *Selected Essays* (1936).

84 For Pollard's significance and the impact of anti-'Whig' sentiment generally, see Blaas 1978: 274–344.

85 John Forster, barrister (1812–76). He was best known to Victorians for his lives of Goldsmith and Dickens, but Gardiner is thinking here presumably of the early biographical studies of Pym, Vane and Eliot (all published in 1831) and his life of *Oliver Cromwell 1599–1658* (1839).

A facile answer might rely on Britain's political and economic supremacy in the nineteenth century and see in historical constitution-alism a simple enjoyment of its status through a relishing of its past.[86] One might speak, less clumsily, of the awareness of a distinctive antiquity surrounding the British polity and the resolution by 1800 of those assimilative problems in regard to Scotland, Wales and Ireland with whose analogues countries like Germany, Italy and Belgium had only recently come to terms. Nineteenth-century historians were willing to see the British *state* appearing as long ago as the thirteenth century and to focus their work on a concept that would have struck an Italian or Belgian as fanciful in respect of his own state. Certainly this line of thought gives a clue; but one can take it further. Perhaps British historiography took its constitutional turn from a sense common to many of its adherents that in writing the history of the state they *were* writing precisely the kind of history that later times deem absent: a form of indirect social history. For men such as Stubbs, the attraction of law and constitutional practice lay in their ability to reflect the lives of thousands of anonymous people and thus provide access to those who could never be reached via direct oral testimony. One can sense in him a 'fascination with the structures fabricated, coral-like, by countless almost imperceptible creatures'. (Burrow 1981: 107). In this sense the constitutional history so despised by twentieth-century social historians had attempted to embrace society by absorbing it into the history of the state. It followed that a radical social history would only emerge in Britain when the pretensions of the state as an avatar of social harmony came into question after 1914.

---

86 Some of this message appears in Martin Wiener's account of *English Culture and the Decline of the Industrial Spirit* (1985).

8

TOWARDS AN HISTORICAL 'PROFESSION'

We are entitled to retain the quotation marks until some point after the First World War. The years from 1860 to 1914 saw considerable change none the less and an observer surveying the background, working conditions, sources, production, expectations and theoretical sophistication of Western historians on the eve of Sarajevo could hardly miss significant developments engendered over the past half-century. Leisured dilettantes who held university posts by virtue of their birth or in spite of their reluctance to prosecute 'research' had decreased as a proportion of the whole. In England one was less likely to run into a Buckle on his daily constitutional or on the way to his club, though one might well encounter Frederick York Powell (1850–1904) on his way to a boxing match as late as the 1890s. Indeed York Powell confutes many suppositions about professionalization understood as a process among historians. As Regius Professor at Oxford he struck the fastidious R. L. Poole as betraying 'an excessive hostility to all things German, an awkward archaic style, and an extreme dilatoriness in carrying out engagements'.[87] Doubtless the impression had gained some currency through his having arrived late for his own inaugural lecture which he had then failed to protract beyond twenty minutes

---

87 R. L. Poole to Lord Acton, 25 Oct. 1896, in Blaas 64 n. 253.

(Slee 1986: 142). And of course once the mind sets out on this track, the quaintnesses rush into view: 'Sligger' Urquart of Balliol College, Oxford, and his chic reading holidays for attractive young men in his Swiss chalet; Oscar Browning of King's College, Cambridge, and his violence against the idea of research; Acton himself who insisted on research while avoiding publishing much of it and whose career had been built on an expensive personal library, an eccentric education at the hands of Dr Döllinger in Germany and the social cachet that helped him become Earl Granville's son-in-law.[88] Even in America, where the *idea* of treating the past in a 'professional' way had entwined itself with a peculiar doctrine about 'objectivity', the main strides in recruiting historians from those of non-notable background had still to come. Peter Novick's recent examination of American historians reveals, for example, that around a quarter of them still came from 'privileged' backgrounds before 1914 (Novick 1988: 171). The thought brings back a wonderful New Year's Resolution – George Bancroft's on the first day of 1821. 'I think it would be highly useful', he wrote in his diary, 'to take lessons in dancing for the sake of wearing off all awkwardness and uncouthness' (Howe 1908: I, 94). Social mobility mattered then far more than professional ascendancy.

While thinking about sociological tendencies among historians, perhaps we do better, indeed, to consider age rather than class or status as a guide to change. For what is apparent in the generation maturing by 1900 is the boost given to the young by the development of the university system in many Western countries and by the spread of the research thesis as both an academic rite of passage and a first rung on the ladder of publication. In France a veritable 'revanche de la jeunesse' seems evident in retrospect.[89] Both there and in America, new opportunities opened before those with the talent to seize them:

---

88 For Urquart, see Bailey 1936. Cf. Browning 1910. Acton has a rough ride in Kenyon 1983; but then Kenyon's account has had a rough ride. Ironically, when Mandell Creighton declared himself pleased that Acton would collaborate on the project that would become the *English Historical Review*, he plainly thought that Acton would supply some professionalism. 'We must confess that we are not strong on historical method in England. Our work has all the advantages and all the disadvantages of amateur work' Creighton 1904: I, 334.

89 The phrase comes from Charles-Olivier Carbonell's important study of French

Before 1914 the professionalization of history [in America] had served as a dramatically successful ladder of personal social and economic mobility for dozens of small-town boys of lower-middle class backgrounds. In the rapidly expanding university world of prewar America, it was not unusual for a bright young man to become a full professor within a few years of receiving the doctorate, and to achieve national eminence before he was out of his thirties. Salaries, for the most successful, compared favourably with those of many other professionals. In the more difficult to measure area of status, the college professor was a figure of consequence in the local community.

(Novick 1988: 169)

Carbonell finds in the French case, similarly, that the *thèse* helped generate historical scholars who, before they were 30, had achieved their first step in a professional world and written a text that would become their first book or series of articles. (Carbonell 1976: 172). On the other hand, the intellectual substance of the Ph.D. qualification, then as now, soon becomes inflated. It helps perspective to recall that Michelet's thesis had amounted to 26 pages of generously spaced text, or to bring to mind Edward Channing's much later Harvard Ph.D. which took eighteen months to produce and comprised 78 pages of unintelligible handwriting (ibid. 265; Novik 1988: 265). Still, with the American universities alone turning out more than 200 of them each year by 1900, the doctoral graduates presented a new feature of an increasingly professional scene and had in effect made the doctorate a precondition of appointment to many university and college posts. First-degree graduates enjoyed a parallel expansion in their number. The Honours school at Oxford expected to see over 100 candidates graduating each year – far larger than the twenty-odd at Cambridge but minuscule in comparison with the 1,000 students of history registered at the Sorbonne by the turn of the century.[90]

A few years earlier, one would have looked less to the University of Paris than to Berlin, Göttingen, Leipzig, Munich, Kiel and Jena for such statistics. The German universities easily outranked French institutions up to the 1880s as vehicles for teaching history. In 1878, for example, there were still only two chairs in history at the Sorbonne, as

historians in the 1860s and 1870s. 'Une vocation les appelle, parfois à l'origine d'un métier.' See his *Histoire et Historiens* (1976): 170.

90 Slee 1986: 125. For the Sorbonne, see Gerard 1983: 81.

opposed to eight each in Berlin and Leipzig (Keylor 1975). Indeed, much of the apparatus of professionalism, from social status to professional journals and attitudes to source-criticism, seemingly began in Germany and then spread outwards. Appearances may deceive, however, and it should be stressed that the German case presents substantial ambiguity. Youth, for example, achieved less rapid advancement there because of the two-tier doctoral system which required not only the normal doctorate, often under the impress of a near-feudal *Doktorvater*, but the more demanding *Habilitation* which made it harder for those under 30 to achieve the meteoric careers sometimes seen in the United States. On the other hand, the availability of junior posts for historians in the system of *Privatdozenten* enabled talented younger people to achieve employment and a salary. Again, structural considerations of this kind sometimes camouflage the degree to which the German norms of co-option and promotion could turn on nepotism and the need to find a powerful patron. The ambiguities soon appear if one reflects on the career of one of the greatest 'professional' historians of the nineteenth century.

Theodor Mommsen's life, after all, spanned most of it: he had reached his mid-eighties when he died in 1903. He achieved, even more than Ranke, the professional dream by out-writing everyone around him. Yet Mommsen's struggles to reach Berlin and the character of his work thereafter comment on the limits of 'professionalization' as a process. He came from Schleswig, the son of a pastor, as so often among German historians, and following his schooling in Altona went to his *Heimatuniversität* at Kiel where he read law and came into contact with Gustav Droysen, Georg Waitz and in particular Otto Jahn.[91] His doctorate in 1843 opened no academic doors; he elected to become a schoolteacher in a girls' school in his home town. It was the serendipity of a royal appointment as Master of Latin Inscriptions that took him on his three years of travel in France and Italy between 1844 and 1847 and which formed the foundation of his epochal work on Roman history. But when his mission ended, he still had no job and went back to teaching schoolchildren, a fate from which the offer of a chair in

---

91 Otto Jahn (1813–69). Principally interested in archaeology and classical philology but also a distinguished musicologist.

jurisprudence at Leipzig rescued him, but only because Jahn had used his influence to prompt it. The appointment went wrong almost at once. Mommsen had more on his mind than jurisprudence in 1848 and so did his employers. His liberalism and support for the new political mood soon sent him elsewhere: to Zurich for a while and then Breslau. So he was 41 before a chance of moving to Berlin arose in the editorship of the *Corpus Inscriptionum Latinarum*; and 44 before he became professor of ancient history at the university there. Once having arrived, his academic output became astonishing in the fields of Roman history and law, though the first three volumes of his *Römische Geschichte* had already appeared. His daughter put it down to genius but she reports Mommsen's ominous reply: 'Nein, mein Kind. . . . Ich habe ein Organisationstalent, das ist aber alles.'[92] Whatever the form of his ability, however, there were those then and since who have alleged that Mommsen's method consisted in reading back the ethos of 1848 into the Roman world and discussing imperial Rome as though it were a reflection of Bismarckian Germany (and vice versa), despite his protestations to the contrary.[93]

Mommsen was a scholar of international repute and a political figure of some weight. Waitz, who had taught him, was a great teacher as well as a luminous collaborator of Pertz at the *Monumenta*: he probably exercised more direct influence on recruitment to the profession in the later years of the century. But both men show the significance of a new style of source-criticism and of one strand of German academia during the Wilhelmine period. One can identify others and Otto Hintze (1861–1940) could act as a cameo for one of them. He had sat under both Mommsen and Waitz, not to mention Droysen, Treitschke and a philosopher, Wilhelm Dilthey, who would prove more significant in the twentieth century than anyone at the time understood. A combination of Treitschke and the economic historian Schmoller as supervisers of his *Habilitation* must have left Hintze bifocal; but the economic and social thrust certainly overpowered the nationalistic and although he

---

92 'No, my child . . . I have a talent for organization, but that's all.' Quoted in Kuczynski 1978: 14.
93 Wücher in particular sees him in this light as 'ein viel zu zeitverbundener Mensch': see Wücher 1956. Cf. Mommsen's denial in a letter to Jahn (1854), quoted in Kuczinski 1978: 85.

became known for his history of Prussia, Hintze's work developed affinities with Lamprecht's, while Weber would later prove an influence. Indeed Christian Simon has recently seen the Berlin professoriate as divisible into three groups: the older political historians of the Treitschke stamp; a younger group interested in *Kultur* more widely defined and in the notion of comparative history; and a further section of the younger men, typified in Max Lenz, who absorbed a Diltheyan concept of *Verstehen* (understanding resting on empathy rather than deductive science) and wanted to graft it on to a Rankean sense of source-criticism (Simon 1988: I, 138–9). Possibly Friedrich Meinecke falls into this latter group but if so his presence only underlines the impossibility of effecting precise divisions. Both he and Hintze contributed greatly to German historiography before 1914[94] – Meinecke particularly through his editorship of the *Historische Zeitschrift* from 1895. Both names take one forward also to a darker period when they would feel the weight of what German nationalism might mean.

These various forms of precocity became thinkable in no small degree because the continuity of Germany's higher educational system had not suffered any severe interruption in the wake of the French Revolution. In France the universities could hardly have suffered more. Abolished by the revolutionaries, they made a limited re-appearance under Napoleon in 1808 as *facultés* which had a social as much as an academic function in offering courses open to the public and lacking any infrastructure on the German model. Only after the coming of the Third Republic in 1871 did the pace of change begin to increase; but – the crucial point – once having begun, it increased exponentially and soon placed France ahead of Germany in the construction of an historical profession. In 1877 the establishment of a new post, the *maître de conférences*, gave young French historians the chance of obtaining positions similar to the *Privatdozenten* in Germany, while the Ferry ministry's introduction of the *agrégation* in history (1881) produced a first-degree structure to rival that of competitor countries. In 1896

---

94 Otto Hintze wrote predominantly on Prussia and the Hohenzollerns: see esp. his *Hohenzollern in ihr Werk* (5th edn, Berlin (1915)). Meinecke's early work examined elements of *Staatsgeschichte* though he turned to historiography in his influential *Rise of Historism* (*Die Entstehung des Historismus*) (1936) and after the war reflected courageously on *Die deutsche Katastrophe* (1946).

'universities' returned. By 1903 the *Ecole des Chartes*, the *Ecole Pratique des Hautes Etudes* and the *Ecole Normale Supérieure* had become part of the University of Paris. The complex of institutions in Paris proved able to mount each year at least fifty courses in history by the early 1880s.[95] Nor did significant change limit itself to expansion. Qualitative shifts also became apparent in the French writing of history from the 1860s. The German approach to textual analysis and apparatus made a clear impact, not least through the example of those who, like Gabriel Monod, had spent time working in Germany. Their editions started to *look* German:

> ces gros livres prennent l'allure savante que leur donnent les longues et prudentes préfaces, le scrupuleux apparat critique qui dévore le rez-de-chaussée, les index et autres outils de travail.
>
> En trente ans, on est passé de l'édition passive, simple copie et paresseuse réproduction, à l'édition critique . . . et pratique.
>
> (Carbonell 1976: 116)

The new rigour informed Monod's *Revue Historique* of 1876 whose much-quoted manifesto is often taken as a significant departure in Western historiography generally but which might more plausibly be seen as a counterblast to the rival *Zeitschrift* of 1859.[96] It committed itself to the conception of scientific history that had dominated French historical thought since the Enlightenment. More importantly, it found itself over the next thirty years operating as a critical forum for discussion of how to teach the subject. When Monod looked back on the journal in 1907 he discovered that he had included no less than thirty-seven articles dealing with some aspect of teaching (Gerard 1983: 80).

If this tendency distanced French experience from the German one, so did the relative conservatism of its preferred historical subject matter. It shared, to be sure, an entire generation's fascination with the ancient world – one in which the republican aspirations of France, the imperial certainties of Germany and the effortless absence of mind celebrated in England could all find some reflection. Carbonell's sample of historical works published in France between 1866 and 1875 suggests that well over half concerned themselves with antiquity,

---

95 For all these developments, see the very helpful exposition of Keylor 1975.
96 For these and other journals of the period, see Stieg 1986.

broadly defined (Carbonell 1976: 269). They also show, however, a far stronger presence of religion in their content than might have been guessed in a culture so committed to analysis. Of that economic history so prominently displayed in the school of Knies, Roscher and others in Germany, there seems comparatively little. More evident is the weight accorded to geography as the true ancillary domain of the historian. This close *Zusammenhang* reached the young at an early point in their education and often continued into the university, as it did with notable effects in the history/geography syllabus followed by the young Marc Bloch at the *Ecole Normale* in the 1900s. It persisted via the scattered documentation of French history which perhaps helped engender a concentration on the region as a focus of study – not quite in the formalized fashion followed in German *Landesgeschichte* but a pervasive tradition none the less.

Where Germany and France had led, England followed but slowly and with a distinctive twist. The singular relationship between class structure and educational opportunity continued to starve the universities of talent from those born to unprivileged parents. To speak of a historical profession committed to teaching in the 1860s may be arguable for Oxford (Slee 1986: 100–2) but it seems unpersuasive as an overall picture. Plainly the reforms imposed on Oxford and Cambridge in the second half of the nineteenth century went some way to developing a new sense of purpose. Certainly the foundation of the *English Historical Review* in 1886 marked an important staging-post in the transformation of professional attitude: its first number printed pieces of considerable distinction from men well known across Europe. The expansion of the university system in a context of economic downturn after the mid-1870s also acted as a catalyst in providing a career structure for those unsuccessful in or stifled by the competition in Oxford and Cambridge. London may have lacked a *Monumenta* or an *Ecole des Chartes* but her centralized public records had the greatest continuity in Europe. Eventual governmental interference in their management, of which the Public Records Act of 1838 was symptomatic (see also Martin and Spufford 1990), and improved access to primary-source collections helped fuel a concern for precise scholarship of the kind practised by Round and encouraged the annihilation of imprecise scholars also practised by Round. Yet by 1900 the model for precise historical work was best embodied in Maitland, whose background hardly emphasized the contours of a self-conscious profession, bringing, like Mommsen, a training in the law to history rather than any steeping in a common training or social catchment. The Royal Historical Society, which theoretically united disparate elements after 1869, in fact acted as a loose manifold for a collection of isolated notables interested mainly in the editing and printing of frequently arcane primary sources.

In those countries where the university system remained nascent, the individuals who wrote history suffered far greater isolation. Spain and Italy present examples where the twentieth century has thrown up far more distinguished historians than did the nineteenth. Spain had its own move towards a systematization of educational institutions, as in the *Institución Libre de Enseñanza* (Free Institute of Education) in 1876. But Spanish universities entered their era of major development only in the first third of the twentieth century, stimulated by what Julian Marías has called the 'tectonic' effect of the lost war against America in 1898 (Marías 1990: 380–4). One finds there significant 'researchers' such as Ramón Menéndez Pidal[97] rather than a school of history. Spaniards in the twentieth century, especially during their crisis of identity in the 1930s, turned back to nineteenth-century authors such as Menendez y Pelayo for their home truths. 'On the subject of the essence or genius of Spain,' Peter Linehan writes,

> a Spain forever stuck in the sixteenth century, a Spain oblivious of the disasters caused by 'bad Spaniards' from 1640 to 1898 and beyond, Menendez y Pelayo was inexhaustible. In 1910, towards the end of his life, he had lamented in words which were to become famous what he called 'the slow suicide' of the Spanish people.
>
> (Linehan 1992: I, 11–12)

Likewise in Italy, the developments we have been considering in northern Europe were not replicated until after 1914 and even then the notion of a 'professional' history sits uncomfortably within the Italian university system. Not that this most historical of cultures failed to make major contributions to historical thought in the revised Idealism associated with Benedetto Croce. Nor was it without distinguished

---

97 Pidal covered almost all aspects of Spanish culture in a wide-ranging *œuvre*. For historians, the most significant are his *Historia de España* (4 vols, 1940–54) and his earlier study of *La España del Cid* (2 vols, Madrid, 1929).

historians, though the acid of fascism corroded the vision and achievement not only of those who embraced it, among whom Volpe stood supreme,[98] but also of those who, like Salvemini, found their careers destroyed because of their opposition, as we shall see later. But the point at issue is a different one. Despite the work of particular individuals, Italian historiography does not reflect the pattern found further north. It required a Ranke to write the history of their popes, a Burckhardt to celebrate their art. Perhaps Italian self-identity was too young a phenomenon and her state-formation too retarded to permit an easy transition to a professionalized packaging of her past. Yet here and in Spain and in tsarist Russia, no sooner had that transition become feasible than state-formation rolled forward at spectacular speed, crushing the resistance of all before it and re-writing accounts of all behind it.

---

98 Gioachimo Volpe (1876–1971). Professor of Modern History, Milan 1905–24; Rome 1924–40. Official historian of the regime: *Storia del movimento fascista* (1939). He had begun as a medievalist (*Eretici e moti ereticali sociale dal XI al XIV secolo* (1907), but then wrote on modern Italian political and diplomatic history, as in his study of *Guerra, Dopoguerra, Fascismo* (1928). After the collapse of fascism he wrote a two-volume account of *L'Italia moderna* (1943–52). For perspectives on post-war Italian historiography, see Bentley 1997, ch. 22.

9

CRISIS OVER METHOD

Radical approaches to history depended to some extent on the burgeoning professionalization of the discipline because a systematic understanding of source materials helped generate new questions about their use and limitations. But larger developments played their part, too. The growth and new concentrations of population in cities, the scale of immigration into the United States in particular, the pace of industrialization in North America and western Europe after 1850, the shrinkage of the world in space and time[99] – these implications of a mass society caught in a period of technological turmoil could not escape historians looking for interesting ways to think about the past. The new context implied that economic issues had lain for too long at the margin of enquiry. It asked how the histories of economies and the social groupings that interacted with them should be constructed. It raised with renewed force the Enlightenment's questions about history's relation to social science. Nor did historians need to frame all their own questions *ab initio*. For the second half of the nineteenth century became so heated with argument about social theory that even if historians had never read a word of Marx or Dilthey or Pareto or Durkheim or Weber, even if they had turned their backs on the sour

---

99 For a stimulating introduction to this theme, see Kern 1983.

Methodenstreit which so disfigured German historical discussion in the 1890s, they could hardly remain immune from the contagion of self-awareness and self-criticism which infected most areas of intellectual enquiry.[100] It did not help those seeking isolation that they comprised the last generation of universalists who expected to find the time to read about the latest developments in biology and geology, physics and philosophy as well as to sustain their historical projects. Epidemics travelled quickly.

We have to ask why a sensitive observer like Lamprecht had become convinced by 1896 that issues of method, rather than wider outlook or assumption, had divided historians into two armed camps.[101] The question takes one back to mid-century and the role that German Idealism had come to play in historical writing, on the one hand, against the claims of science, voiced especially in France, on the other. In the wake of Darwinist argument among social theorists and internal developments within inductive science itself, those latter claims gained ground in the 1870s and 1880s. Perhaps scientific approaches did not often translate in a literal way: the past offers few laboratories. But the need to categorize, systematize and above all to *reduce* became paramount in a culture bewildered by its own volume. Reduction took a number of forms but one motif ran through much of it. The past became, as it had been in *dix-huitième* Paris, a series of predictable transitions organized less as a finite number of ages in the style of Vico or Condorcet than as a progression from one conceptual state to another. For Sir Henry Maine, whose *Ancient Law* (1861) attracted widespread notice in Britain, the journey through time witnessed a transition from a society based on status to one based on contract.[102] For Herbert Spencer, Maine's contemporary, it reflected a universal grain in organic and inorganic matter that required an unstable condition of homogeneity always to differentiate itself over time into a more sophisticated and permanent one of heterogeneity; and that process inhered in everything from the evolution of the galaxy to the

---

100 See the seminal, though now dated, analysis of Hughes 1959.

101 . . . 'ein Unterschied der Methode, nicht der Weltanschauung, . . . der die Vertreter des Faches in zwei Heerlager spaltet' (*Alte und neue Richtungen* (1896): 4).

102 Maine 1861. The longest chapter in the account is on 'The Early History of Contract', pp. 252–304.

organization of the brain and the social division of labour.[103] For the German sociologist Tönnies the journey for all societies wound through a landscape always dominated by the conceptual norms of *Gemeinschaft* on the one side and *Gesellschaft* on the other with the latter producing the stronger polarity.[104] And of course each of these progressions anticipated or echoed in some way the more famous, but more catastrophic, transitions envisaged by Marx.

It seems paradoxical that the theorist who shaped historical thinking more than any of his contemporaries should never have written any substantial history himself, unless *Das Kapital* (which began to appear in German in 1867 and was translated into English in 1887) be conceived as an implied history of industrial society. We have 'The Eighteenth Brumaire of Louis Bonaparte' as one example of the style and a series of forceful theoretical postulates in the preface to the *Critique of Political Economy* of 1859. Yet for the most part Marx's view of historical change remains a retrospective construction that continues to engross his theologians and critics.[105] His retention of the Hegelian dialectic as a fundamental explanation of change and his turning of it 'downside up' by grounding the dialectic in correspondences and frictions between the forces of production and the relations of production offered a new way of conceiving how societies worked:

> In the social production which men carry on they enter into definite relations that are indispensable and independent of their will; these relations of production correspond to a definite stage of development of their material powers of production. The sum total of these relations of production constitutes the economic structure of society – the real foundation, on which rise legal and political superstructures and to which correspond definite forms of social consciousness. The mode of production in material life determines the general character of the social, political, and spiritual processes of life.

---

103 For Herbert Spencer's ideas, see in particular *Social Statics* (1855) and his *Autobiography* (1904). Among recent commentaries are Peel 1971 and Andreski 1971. For the wider issues in social theory, see Taylor 1992.

104 Ferdinand Tönnies produced a considerable body of writing among which the most indicative for his historical ideas are probably *Gemeinschaft und Gesellschaft* (1926) and *Einführung in die Soziologie* (1931). He can be contextualized through Bickel 1991.

105 For modern assessments, see Rigby 1987 and Cohen 1979. Dr Rigby considers the impact of Marxism on recent historiography in Bentley 1997, ch. 36.

Implicit in this picture of social change one can sense a view of historical processes – almost a programme for the past:

> No social order ever disappears before all the productive forces for which there is room . . . have been developed, and new, higher relations of production never appear before the material conditions of their existence have matured in the womb of the old society.[106]

Phrases such as the 'social order' betokened a radical reorientation of what historians might study and led in that direction for reasons that were to prove of fundamental significance. It was not simply that a new emphasis emerged when 'society' became its own unit of analysis rather than a collective noun for all the individuals who composed it. ('The history of all hitherto existing *society* is the history of class struggles.')[107] Marx's point thrust far deeper. His allegation was that individuals did not make up societies at all. Societies rather made individuals by providing the framework from which they took their meaning. One of the most arresting thoughts in the whole of Marx's writing – certainly one of the most challenging to conventional historical method – emerges in his bald remark that 'society does not consist of individuals; it expresses the sum of connections and relationships in which individuals stand.'[108] This idea was to become an organizing concept for several strains of social theory in the late nineteenth century and the starting-point for new departures in an authentic 'social' history in the twentieth.

In presenting a social theory that reflected Marx's concern with 'social holism' or 'social realism', none took the concept further than the French sociologist Emile Durkheim (1858–1917). Possibly his origins in a Jewish family with long rabbinical traditions increased his sensitivity to societies as living organisms that had the power to dictate what individuals did or thought. He certainly acquired the power to make his own contemporaries do his bidding, especially following his promotion from Bordeaux to Paris in 1902 where he exercised a formidable influence over a generation of research students and

---

106 Both quotations come from the preface to the *Critique of Political Economy*, quoted by R. V. Daniels in Cahnman and Boskoff 1964: 65, 68.
107 The all too well-known first sentence of the *Communist Manifesto* of 1848 (my emphasis).
108 From his *Grundrisse*, quoted in Cohen 1979: 37.

terrorized those whom he failed to persuade. The rival cults of Durkheim and Bergson preoccupied Parisian students in the years before the First World War and each was to bring to historical work a distinctive voice. Like Marx, Durkheim was not a historian but a *soi-disant* 'sociologist'; his reputation had been made in the explication of social variables – suicide, famously, in the 1890s and then, more controversially, religion.[109] He nevertheless legislated for historians by redefining their method until it resembled his own. In a debate with the grotesquely maligned French historian Seignobos, who had co-authored one of the least-loved manuals of historical method in modern times, Durkheim reacted against any attempt to see history and sociology in contrasted categories, 'as if they were two disciplines using different methods'.[110] Historians should approach the history of society in the way sociologists analysed its present: in accordance with major axes along which all social formations could be placed. Here Durkheim outflanked Marx in regarding the social fabric as so 'real' as to empower the observer to speak of its physical attributes, just as a physicist might talk about the gaseous content of a flask – its volume, its concentration, the ability of the molecules to communicate energy to one another. Taken together, these and other attributes enabled the analyst to move away from the 'why?' questions that turned into a request for information about origins, and turn towards those 'how?' questions that would reveal the *function* of variables within a given social system which would in turn throw up a more satisfying understanding of what it is that compels societies to change and present reasons for not seeing their transitions as arbitrary. In order to unearth these functions the historian must analyse those 'coercive' elements in a society's make-up that exercise obvious control and definition over the individual. From 1898 Durkheim referred to such elements as *représentations collectives* and directed students to look for them in

---

109 *Elementary Forms of the Religious Life* appeared in 1912 and presented the thesis that religion should be understood as 'primarily a system of ideas with which individuals represent to themselves the society of which they are members, and the obscure but intimate relations which they have with it'. For a brilliant modern critique of some of the implications for historians, see Bossy 1982.

110 Quoted by R. N. Bellah, in Cahnman and Boskoff 1964: 86. Cf. Langlois and Seignobos 1898; the English translation has a preface by York Powell.

language, group customs and practices, legislation, works of art and literature and, more portentous for the future of historical method, in statistical abstracts free from the contamination of partiality.[111]

The tissue of ideas associated with Durkheim had yet to find an historical application. In Germany the situation was more complicated: practice and theory ran in grooves that sometimes separated but occasionally converged. Not that the Germans lacked ideologues willing to drive theoretical precepts through historical material. Indeed the young Durkheim had gained some of his insights from the wild writings of the pioneer psychologist Wilhelm Wundt (1832–1920). 'Everything occurs mechanically', Wundt had said,[112] and he found many to follow him in his determinism. Most thinkers and researchers looked for a different route, none the less, and in their arguments we can see the beginning of the controversy over method in the humanities that was to dog speculation in Germany for a generation. That this response characterized Germany in particular we may ascribe to two central conditions in German intellectual life. First, the economic surge which characterized the years after 1870 produced a form of economic history which posed important theoretical questions of a kind which, for example, the British school of William Cunningham and W. J. Ashley did not. This assault from 'scientism' in method had to direct itself, second, at the most formidable philosophical establishment in Europe and one which still cleaved to its Idealist heritage. It will help the logic and chronology surrounding these points if we consider them in reverse order.

To a unique extent the purchase of Kantian and Hegelian ideas remained firm in Germany despite the aggression of scientific assumptions and methodologies after 1860. The United States never experienced it, outside a few individuals; the British played with it in their academic philosophy but less so in their histories; the Italians retained significant features of it but diverted much of it into their own special brew of nationalism and Marxism; the French largely eschewed it. When, therefore, Wilhelm Dilthey took his place in Lotze's chair of philosophy in Berlin from 1882 he spoke to an audience considerably

---

111 These aspects of Durkheim's approach are lucidly presented in Lukes 1973.
112 Quoted in Lukes 1973: 91.

larger than the university and to a constituency which, beyond Germany, he would have been denied. Between 1882 and his death in 1911 Dilthey produced a critique of scientific method in its application to the humanities which only now are we fully discovering. Like Vico, he has had to wait a century to receive the reading he requires; and, like Vico, he has become regarded as a father-figure for a number of persuasions among succeeding generations. Since he conceived a particular interest in and sympathy for historical thought, moreover, his ideas invite more than a moment's consideration.

Dilthey's quarry was a special form of inner experience that he called *Erlebnis*. In his early days an exposure to Ranke's seminar and a dose of Buckle had left him convinced that history moved according to laws and was less explanatory when considering the lives of individuals than psychology – a view he retained until about 1894. The breakthrough in his understanding lay in deciding that psychology could not give an account of how individuals revealed their essential selves *over time*; the true psychology was therefore history. But the history could not be that nomothetic or law-based enquiry he had once envisaged. It would need to be ideographic, in Windelband's terminology, certainly; but it ought to be viewed as a discipline in itself, a *Geisteswissenschaft* with its own techniques and assumptions. It would seek not the law-based 'explanation' required in science, but a form of *Verstehen*, by which Dilthey intended not merely 'understanding' but a series of procedures for achieving it. One of them consisted of using one's *own* sense of lived experience to discover it in past figures, to 'locate the I in the Thou'. This sense of historical *Einfühlung* has come into English as 'empathy' and it is now one of the most used, many would say over-used, concepts in the modern teaching of history. 'We understand', Dilthey said,

> when we restore life and breath to the dust of the past out of the depths of our own life. . . . The general psychological condition for this is always present in the imagination; but a thorough understanding of historical development is first achieved when the course of history is re-lived in imagination at the deepest points at which the movement forward takes place.[113]

---

113 Quoted in Plantinga 1980: 109–10.

The last clause has all the blurredness that dogs Dilthey's formulations, but it seems to imply the possibility of using one's vantage point as a historian to observe transformations invisible to contemporaries. Events can be placed in a total continuum: the parts of the story make more sense in the context of the whole, which in turn becomes clearer because one knows the parts better, which in turn gives the whole an expanded perspective, which in turn illuminates other parts, and so on. Dilthey thus invents a dialectical way of thinking about how history can be approached. It is a deeply humanistic account – history is a domain where 'life grasps life' (Dilthey 1976; cf. Rickman 1979) – to which British Idealist thinkers such as Collingwood would respond. And it offered a way for historians to think of their practice as autonomous, even though Dilthey never wrote the Kantian *Critique of Historical Reason* that was going to establish these thoughts in a systematic way.[114]

If such notions recommended one style of method in the *Geisteswissenschaften*, then the school of economic history associated with Knies, Roscher and Schmoller was already employing a very different one. For the use of economic models and the abstractions of economic theory called into question not only the method of Dilthey but the entire genre that they regarded as history. Friedrich Tenbruck well suggests the distance between a discipline based on reviving the inner experience of individual actors and a new one in which such revivals, even when feasible, seemed irrelevant to the project. 'Here', he writes,

> the formless mass of data did not permit an ordering by the traditional methods because what was at issue was a concern with overall conditions (*Zustände*) as opposed to actions. Procedures were therefore developed that worked with 'evolutionary stages' or even 'evolutionary laws' to bring order to the disparate plurality of individual facts.

> (Tenbruck 1987: 236)

For some that distance seemed too far to travel because it blurred the distinction between science, as an environment in which it made sense to speak of regularities and laws, and human behaviour which, if only because of freedom of the will, would always beggar consistency.

---

114 For this theme and for Dilthey generally, see Michael Ermarth's valuable study, *Wilhelm Dilthey: the Critique of Historical Reason* (1978). A recent account is Owensby 1994.

Indeed the so-called *Methodenstreit* opened with a controversy between Gustav Schmoller and Carl Menger which centred on that precise point. Often in intellectual circles a trivial occasion becomes a platform for ideas long in circulation but somehow inarticulate. Some unanticipated enhancement of the kind must have affected a lecture by Wilhelm Windelband who commented on these controversies in 1894 in *Geschichte und Naturwissenschaft*. The separation of subject matter in the humanities into those that rewarded treatment by scientific techniques and those that did not had dominated discussion for a decade. But Windelband invented new words for it and thereby gained immortality. His distinction between 'nomothetic' aspects of reality (those which are subject to the operation of laws and regularities) and 'ideographic' areas where laws do not apply has entered academic language. It was Windelband's lecture that influenced Wundt's colleague at Leipzig, Karl Lamprecht, when he turned against his critics in 1896 after he had been goaded beyond endurance by bitter reviews of the first five volumes of his *Deutsche Geschichte* from a collection of neo-Rankian historians.[115] It was a combination of Windelband and Dilthey that stimulated Heinrich Rickert into defending Idealist history from the attack of science in 1902.

As a teacher of philosophy at Freiburg, Rickert became dismayed through the 1890s at the incursion of 'science' into historical work – dismayed and surprised, as he recalled a decade later:

> In these days ... I would have considered it the least possible of all possibilities that even in historical circles, the old idea of the 'elevation of history to the status of a science' by means of the method of natural science would reappear so soon and prove itself capable of attracting attention; for at that time, the belief in Buckle and related thinkers seemed to be thoroughly discredited in the province of history and retained a role only in naturalistic philosophy. Today, nevertheless, the old speculations of the Enlightenment are treated as the most novel and important achievements of history. For this reason, I thought it necessary to demonstrate the conceptual confusions that lie at the basis of these views ...
>
> (Preface to Rickert [1896] 1986: 4)

---

115 The context of this debate is presented very fully in Chickering 1993: 146–253. Raphael Lutz has seen broad parallels – '[t]hematische Übereinstimmungen und zeitliche Parallelität' – between this debate and what occurred in France when Berr's *Revue de synthèse* raised the issue of nomothetic explanation in the humanities. Cf. Lutz 1990.

His unappealing title – *Die Grenzen der naturwissenschaftlichen Begriffsbildung* – and his less than animated prose perhaps denied Rickert's volume the impact it might have had, for the argument is powerful and often crushing. He regarded concepts as abstracted constructs with no basis in actuality; individual events do not generate such constructs; at the individuated level of analysis it followed that the concepts on which science rested could not reach and explain individual actions and events. There existed, therefore, what he called a *hiatus irrationalis* between concept and reality (ibid. xvi), and it would of necessity remain unbridgeable. These views, reflecting in some respects a Kantian vision of the world, mattered on their own account but they mattered also on a more particular one. Rickert's colleague at Freiburg during the gestation of these ideas was the young economist Max Weber; and Rickert's critique of 'scientism' proved crucial in undermining Weber's juvenile theories and turning his mind towards framing a synthesis of the two dispositions that we have been considering. Indeed, the point of labouring this dialectical swing between two poles of argument has consisted partly in providing an adequate framework within which to understand the importance and contribution of Weber.

By 1904, when Weber entered a two-year period of intense meditation on the problems of methodology, he had grasped the reins of two horses travelling in opposite directions. One of them galloped towards a view of 'social science' that insisted at the very least on the patterning and replicability of human behaviour. The other headed towards a form of individualism that conceded Rickert's neo-Kantian positions about the unknowability of the world in general and individual whim in particular – a position that would always leave a gap between a researcher trying to make sense of social behaviour and the imponderables of individual choice and perception that helped constitute it.[116] Faced with this tension within his thinking – one informed by the specific discussions of method in economics, economic

---

116 The relationship between Weber and Rickert is persuasively analysed by Burger 1976. Although many other studies have been undertaken since Burger's, usually from a sociological or philosophical stance, I have found Burger's study the most helpful for historians since he makes a clear effort to locate Weber's thinking within a precise context of time and space.

history, the philosophy of 'value' and the role of historical enquiry that had dominated German speculation through the 1890s – Weber moved towards a position that maintained the tension rather than eased it and positioned himself within a context quite as *zeitbedingt* as any contemporary writer. With those other writers no subsequent problem has ensued: nobody thinks that Lamprecht or Simmel or Rickert can be understood outside the paradigms of their day. But Weber has been, partly through his own ambition to transcend context, turned into a minor prophet speaking to all ages; he has become dehistoricized. As a consequence critics find fault with Weber's answers without properly understanding the questions that, mostly, were not his in the first place.

He wanted to go beyond both Dilthey and Rickert. Dilthey would not do because his notion of *Verstehen* seemed to Weber a weak, descriptive activity based on individual intuitions that would often prove simply aesthetic. Empathy no doubt helped historians, but empathy was not explanation. Rickert valuably corroded scientistic certainties and showed why a nomothetic concept of social behaviour would not work. But to leave matters there would be to relegate social enquiry to a form of historism in which detailed description of specifics would exhaust the possibilities. His resolution, amended and embattled between 1906 and the appearance of *Wirtschaft und Gesellschaft* at the end of the war, lay in insisting on the importance of *concepts* in social (and therefore historical) thought. Most observers agreed that researchers should look for common characteristics in the phenomena that they studied and try to form classifications – *Klassenbegriffe* – based on those perceptions. These were concepts of a kind; but they were not *gattungsmässig* or generic: they identified common denominators but they did not help over issues of significance and essence. In order to form a view of the world, one had to move beyond what the world itself would yield up in trivial description: one needed a more powerful sense of concept and only the observer could frame it. It was this enriched, authorially generated, organizing concept to which Weber gave the name 'ideal type', which has suffered ever since from the ambiguities inherent in the German understanding of 'ideal' for this generation. Weber's notion had elements of both the Kantian sense of ideal, in that it represented an imposition of mind on the unassimilable complication of the external world, but also of a utopian meaning of the term, for ideal types gave an understanding of how particular individuals, groups or social formations would behave in an ideal world of rationality and consistency. Unravelling the problems of conceiving the relationship between observer and world in this way ultimately passed by or defeated Weber and it has never been fully achieved, though Burger's account dispenses with many problems of *ignoratio elenchi* (see Burger 1976, esp. 115–30). For immediate purposes we need rather to recognize that Weber had devised a methodological instrument, whose use he tried to exemplify in his construction of a model[117] of early modern 'Protestantism' and 'capitalism' in order to show how one implied the other (Weber 1958), on which historians of recent times have seized as a way of manipulating complexity or, not infrequently, providing a safe haven from Marxism.

Between the death of Marx in 1883 and that of Weber in 1920, the place of history in the humanities had shifted and the humanities themselves had undergone redefinition. To one historian in the inter-war period, indeed, it seemed as though Weber and his kind of history had turned into nothing less than sociology (Antoni 1940, 1962). If some historians persisted in the older patterns of thought they did so defensively by 1914. Others were more likely to ask, as Lamprecht had wondered in 1896, where these new movements would take the subject (Lamprecht 1896). Some had already gone further than Lamprecht would ever want to go. Currents would shortly drag on Western historiography in ways that, particularly in America and France, might widen the scope of historical enquiry in ways that would have seemed revolutionary, even arcane, two decades earlier. Reviewing them from a distance of almost a century, it becomes plainer that these radical waves had their own weight and significance but rolled in the grip of a yet stronger tide.

---

117 This is the closest modern term to what Weber had in mind and will suffice for most practical purposes; but readers are reminded that Weber's epistemological position is quite distinct from and considerably more profound than that cheerfully adopted by most of the historians who use it.

10

FROM THE NEW WORLD

As much in historiography as in music, Dvořák's visit to America in 1892 echoed a broadening contact between Europe and the New World. Weber and Schmoller could hardly have missed it when at least one of their pupils in Berlin in the early 1890s had been both American and black. It is not one's first thought about W. E. B. Du Bois: he fits into memory more naturally as part of a fabric of American Negro Marxism woven around Fisk and Harvard, the universities of Pennsylvania and Atlanta (where he developed into the confrontational author of *The Souls of Black Folk* (1903)) and the New York ambience that would later give rise to *Black Reconstruction* (1935).[118] Yet Du Bois's two years in Europe remain important in retrospect for the illumination of a common strand in American graduate experience. One could exemplify it under a less glaring light. Consider John William Burgess, the political scientist who did so much to remodel Columbia University's faculty system in the 1880s but who clung to his Hegelian ideas and became the first Roosevelt Professor in the

---

118 Du Bois (1868–1963) came originally from New England and developed his racial consciousness at Fisk. He later became so embittered over this issue that he renounced his American citizenship and departed in voluntary exile to Ghana, where he died. There is a recent perspective on his racial ideas in Hae-song 1992. Cf. Andrews 1985 and Moore 1981.

University of Berlin in 1906. Or, among historians, recall the two Adamses: Henry Brooks Adams (1838–1918) and Herbert Baxter Adams (1850–1901). The first, as scion of a great Boston family, enjoyed the cosmopolitanism inevitable in one whose grandfather and great-grandfather had held the greatest office in the land; and doubtless felt driven by a similar imperative to write the histories of formative administrations in the American past – volumes of careful scholarship that American historians still see as the pillar of his historical writing (Henry Brooks Adams 1889–90). For others the masterpiece of *Mont-Saint-Michel and Chartres*, which did not appear until 1904, his Grand Tour, after Harvard, at the end of the 1850s and his commuting between Washington and Paris from the 1880s enabled him to stamp a particular European influence on those around him, even if his tenure of a university chair had been a short one and his subsequent life broken by events that he excised from his famous autobiography.[119] The second Adams, also a New Englander, brought to his post-doctoral appointment at Johns Hopkins in 1876 the fruits of two years in Heidelberg and Berlin, a questionable regard for his *Doktorvater*, an energizing earnestness about the German seminar system and a dangerous historical theory about Teutonic dissemination.[120]

American students went to Germany in order to pursue doctoral work because before 1880 they had very little choice. When Baxter Adams went to Johns Hopkins on his return from Germany, he joined the first graduate school in history in the United States. Columbia's in New York had stuck at the planning stage for a number of years; it opened only in 1880–1. Gradually the pull of German academia lost its strength in the last two decades of the century. There were those, certainly, who continued the tradition after the need for it had disappeared: witness the man most credited with the origins of a 'new

---

119 *The Education of Henry Adams* (1917) omits, among many other things, his marriage into a family of depressives and the subsequent suicide of his wife following the death of her father in 1885.

120 Baxter Adams retained his faith in the 'germ theory' which assumed the dissemination of the *Markgenossenschaft* into modern Western institutions. Cf. his *The Germanic Origins of New England Towns* (1882). His devotion to Johann Kaspar Bluntschli led to a privately printed memoir.

history' in America, James Harvey Robinson (1863–1936). He could have remained in the United States after graduating from Harvard but a combination of private means and *Wanderlust* took him to Freiburg where he worked with the constitutional historian Hermann E. von Holst who later himself moved to America. Robinson returned to appointments at the University of Pennsylvania and later Columbia with an admiration for Lamprecht and a devotion to German techniques of source-criticism that he imposed on his students. He therefore fits an older model, but variants in the year-abroad syndrome become apparent as one examines others. The rampant radical Charles Beard went to (of all places) Oxford and was supervised by (of all people) York Powell. Charles Haskins, the prodigy who entered college at 13, graduated at 17 and took his Ph.D. at Johns Hopkins at 19, went to both Berlin and Paris but gained more from Langlois and Lot, as his future research interest in Normandy would imply. Carl Becker, Beard's moderate twin, embraced the new model by going nowhere at all: Wisconsin, *cum* Turner and Haskins, Columbia, *cum* Robinson, and then into his first post at Pennsylvania State University on a career that would wind through Kansas and Minnesota to Cornell.

Becker and his inspirational teacher, Frederick Jackson Turner, help suggest through the distinctiveness of their backgrounds an important new sociology among those born into the era of Reconstruction. Turner instantiated his own thesis about the frontier. His parents had come from traditional New England stock but his father had gone west, to Portage, Wisconsin, where he ultimately became owner of the local newspaper and instilled in his son a regard for things American in their own right rather than as copies from a European original. Turner never lost that sense of aggression, as Becker recalled:

> If he knew that Europe was infinitely richer than the United States in historic remains and traditions, I never heard him mention the fact. . . . It was as if some rank American flavor . . . kept the man still proud to be an American citizen, contentedly dwelling in Madison, quite satisfied with the privilege of going every day to the State Historical Society Library where the Draper Manuscripts were.
>
> (Becker 1935: 11)

Becker and Beard reinforce the trend away from the Atlantic and towards the Midwest. Both were brought up on farms, Becker in Iowa, Beard in Indiana. James Harvey Robinson's father reflected the social prestige of banking and left his son with private means; yet Robinson, too, originated not in New England but in Bloomington, Illinois. Add Haskins's connection with Meadville, Pennsylvania, and a tendency becomes sufficiently clear. The 'middle group' of American historians – those sandwiched between the pioneers and the young Turks of the *fin-de-siècle* – had headed for Harvard as a matter of course: George Bancroft, John Lothrop Motley, Francis Parkman and William H. Prescott all fitted this model (see Novick 1988: 72–3; cf. Bassett 1917). Their work had striven for the heroic treatment of heroic themes and evolved into a literary formalism redolent of the English romantic school. The new generation looked elsewhere, if not to the textual analysis familiar in German seminars then to the slogans of Freeman and Acton or the inner pulse of American experience with acknowledgement to no one.

The latter diagnosis came first. But then Turner (1861–1932), who effected it, was a couple of years older than James Harvey Robinson (1863–1936) and escaped the complications of a European entanglement. He left his undergraduate university (Wisconsin) only for a short period at Johns Hopkins and by the age of 28 had rejoined Wisconsin as an assistant professor. In completing his apprenticeship so quickly by American standards he gave himself the opportunity of benefiting intellectually from the census of 1890, one of whose conclusions he was about to place before the historical public as a major structural change in American society. For this census could be interpreted to imply the closure of the American frontier and the removal of what Turner had come to see as the most important single feature of American democracy and character: the availability of a new world to conquer and the transforming consequences for those who tried. Life on the boundary of the known world had thrown up unique challenges and met with responses whose story should be seen as the spine of American history. Other elements played their role, naturally; but the frontier had supplied the decisive factor, the catalyst that made American society distinctive and that held the key to understanding its past. The argument seems not to have impressed those who heard it in Chicago in 1893. Thirty years later a schoolboy historian could hardly avoid coming across 'The Frontier in American History'[121] or escape the sense of breakthrough

121 The lecture is reprinted in *The Frontier in American History* (1921).

that accompanied the idea's popularity. It was not Turner's only idea, for he had two. A second major thesis turned on sectionalism: the clash of regional and sociological cultures and interest groups – which Turner alleged had complemented the frontier in providing an explanation for the track of American experience (Turner 1932). All the same, his career remained one of promise unfulfilled, short not only on published work but on imaginative fluidity because of his penchant for patterns and schemata. But his teaching struck those who received it as special in its quality and openness. Among its most prominent beneficiaries was a scholar who would shrink from schemata and develop his own hesitations about method.

Whether the Carl Becker who made the journey to Madison in 1893 ever resembled the 'prairie country boy' he liked to recall in later years (Becker 1935: 191), it brooks no denial that he came to admire Frederick Turner intensely and to share his dismissiveness over theoretical nit-picking and Europhilia. Becker's homespun quality has two sorts of camouflage: his concern with intellectual history and his famous scepticism about historical 'fact' that was to link him with Beard's relativism in the 1930s.[122] Both of these attributes had appeared before the First World War. His doctoral thesis had dealt with American political parties in New York (Becker 1901), without any intimations of that 'new' history which he always considered merely the latest of many fashions. By the time of his first general book, *The Beginnings of the American People* in 1915, he had espoused the frontier as a major part of the explanatory apparatus (Becker 1915: 180–1, 184) and had also begun to grope his way towards what he would later call, after Whitehead, a climate of opinion. For the moment it came out in isolated remarks which tried to fix *mentalité* in a diffuse phrase, as when he doubted whether colonial aristocrats 'had permitted the dissolvent philosophy of the century to enter the very pith and fiber of their mental quality' (ibid. 171). There was no suggestion that this pith and fibre lay beyond recovery, for all those initial doubts about factuality that had emerged in an article of 1910. (Becker 1935: 1–34) He retained a belief in the possibility of

---

122 For an introduction, see Dray 1980. The issue of relativism and the place of Becker and Beard within it preoccupies much of Peter Novick's analysis of the inter-war period in Novick 1988, esp. 250ff.

'imaginative reconstruction of vanished events' (Becker 1932: 88) long after he had disproved for himself the coherence of the 'facts' which the 'reconstruction' would require. This awkwardness does not argue that Becker's views about factuality were trivial (though in comparison with, say, Oakeshott's systematic treatment of the issue they certainly look amateur).[123] It rather implies that 'the objectivity question' may not have so much edge on it in Becker's case than observers imagine. His affinity to Turner's starting-points and his antipathy to all 'new' or 'scientific' history, even to the idea of historiography itself ('labelling'), come closer to the core. He would have regarded this paragraph about him as not so much a criticism as an intrusion on intellectual privacy.

Harry Elmer Barnes, who wrote a distinguished account of modern historiography, stung Becker repeatedly by counting him among the New Historians in whose novelty Becker disbelieved (see Barnes 1962: 373ff.; Becker 1935a, esp. 36–40; cf. Becker 1935b: 132–42). The laurel rested better on Robinson and Beard. They had collaborated at Columbia, once Beard had finished his Ph.D. in 1904, on a textbook covering modern European history (Robinson and Beard 1907–8) and contrived to present an account that spent less time on political history than conventional books in order to treat 'the more fundamental economic matters' (ibid. I, 4). In practice this meant that Beard would be allowed to write a polemical piece at the end about Marx, social reform, trade unions, Booth, Rowntree and the paraphernalia of Ruskinism with which Beard had surrounded himself in Manchester and London during his bad-tempered stay in England. Apart from that, the book had eight pages on English trade in the eighteenth century, ten on science and a twelve-page chapter in volume 2 on the Industrial Revolution. This hardly made a manifesto for Weber. Indeed, the opening lament that 'our historical manuals . . . have ordinarily failed to connect the past with the present' (ibid. I, iii) sounded more like an invocation of Freeman. It was rather Robinson's *The New History* of 1912 that placed the message in a more European key,

---

123 Michael Oakeshott, *Experience and its Modes* (1932) appeared in the same year as Becker's Storrs Lectures on the eighteenth century (see Becker 1932) and assaulted common-sense understanding of factuality from an explicitly Idealist direction, whereas Becker left behind a probably inadvertent Kantianism for others to find. See Smith 1956: 53–4.

though the volume has a slighter feel than its reputation might imply. Most of the 'manifesto' was announced through a short, introductory essay in a volume that collected together a number of disparate papers. Its burdens were four: that historians should broaden the terms of their enquiry and move away from a narrow political history; that they should seek what Robinson called a 'genetic' approach to their problems, pressing back causation through time, seeking the oak in the acorn, as it were; that they should, third, apply the tools developed within the various social sciences to historical enquiry and seek to blur the boundaries of the subject with sociology, psychology, economics and so on; and lastly – a point seized on later by Richard Hofstadter – that historians should make their subject an instrument for social progress (Robinson 1912; cf. Hofstadter 1968).

Yet the 'new history' as an American genre never quite happened. 'I waited hopefully', Becker once reminisced, 'for the appearance of one of these new histories . . . None appeared.' (Becker 1935a: 36–7). It was not that Robinson, for one, swerved away from his commitment so much as that he read into the changed conditions of post-war America different imperatives – the same ones seen by Becker. All had become new and changed; the world of Einstein and Eddington and Jeans and Whitehead had established the wonder, but also the tyranny, of fact, just as President Harding's normalcy had reified the American dream of business. One's priority lay in transcending both with an expanded sense of mind:

> So novel are the conditions, so copious the knowledge, that we must under-take the arduous task of reconsidering a great part of the opinions about man and his relations to his fellow-men which have been handed down to us by previous generations who lived in far other conditions and possessed far less information about the world and themselves. We have, however, first to create an *unprecedented attitude of mind to cope with unprecedented conditions and to utilize unprecedented knowledge*.[124]

---

124 Robinson 1921: 4–5 (emphasis in original). For business, see ibid. 173. Robinson's book became a best-seller. Compare Becker's complaint against positivist ideas about 'facts', presented as a description of the post-war intellectual environment: 'We start with the irreducible brute fact, and we must take it as we find it, since it is no longer permitted to coax or cajole it, hoping to fit it into some or other category of thought on the assumption that the pattern of the world is a logical one. Accepting the fact as given, we observe it, experiment with it, verify it, classify it, measure it if possible, and reason

But this programme produced in Robinson a series of books that had less to do with history than with cosmology. He sought to replace conventional understandings of change over time by a general morphology of the kind developed by Oswald Spengler whose criticisms of modern historians Robinson came to accept. 'They have told how things *have been*,' he argued in his italicized way, 'rather than how they *came about*' (Robinson 1937: 11). Retailing how they came about left him sounding metaphysical and windy. Then he developed mental blocks, apparently, and finished few of the projects he set himself in later life. There persists in his post-war work a sense of *diminuendo*.

His erstwhile collaborator, Charles Beard, never knew this mood: his sole alternative to *forte* had long been *fortissimo*. His 'new history' developed its own theme after 1912 and it turned not on mind but on capitalism. In effect, the Beards (for Mary Beard contributed as a significant historian in her own right) wrote a three-volume history of economic causes and consequences in American history from the 1770s to the industrialization of the nineteenth century (Beard and Beard 1913; 1915; 1927). Of these the first remains memorable for the outrage it provoked. *An Economic Interpretation of the Constitution* offended through the directness of its prose but also because people read it as a rubbishing of the American heritage hidden within a tight and logical exposition. Property in the eighteenth century fell under two heads: 'realty', by which Beard meant authentic landholding by farmers, and 'personalty', by which he wanted to identify speculation for gain; the latter group believed their interests compromised by the Articles of Confederation and they supplied the central figures of the Constitutional Convention of 1787 since they benefited from an absurdly small electorate among white males. In their hands the new Constitution became, inevitably, an expression of particular anxieties and purposes which married democratic argument to economic interest. 'The Constitution was essentially an economic document based upon the concept that the fundamental rights of property are anterior to government and morally beyond the reach of popular majorities' (Beard and Beard 1913: 324). It was 'essentially' so because

---

about it as little as may be. The questions we ask are "What?" and "How?" . . . Our supreme object is to measure and master the world rather than to understand it.' (Becker 1932: 16–17).

'great movements in politics' were understood generally as suffering conditioning by 'real economic forces' (ibid. v). Had Beard remained central to the academic historical establishment, his message might perhaps have escaped the marginalization it encountered after the First World War. His courageous resignation from Columbia in 1917, when he refused to accept the treatment handed out to faculty members who opposed the war, rendered this impossible and he drifted into the role of a non-Marxist *enfant terrible*, an existence eased after he inherited his father's money and bought a large house at New Milford, Connecticut, from where he could scream dissent like an American Jacobin or score clever points in the manner of Sidney Smith.

If, indeed, anyone succeeded in implementing a new history after 1918, the only candidate strong enough would be one who eschewed the manifestos of 1907–13, who continued his annual visits to Europe through that period, patiently amassing a mastery of Norman and English archives and whose critical contribution to the understanding of *Norman Institutions* (1918) still commanded a readership half a century later. And the significance of Charles Homer Haskins went further as his interests and expertise widened to include the twelfth-century Renaissance and the medieval university (Haskins 1923; 1927). Prominent though Haskins's history remains in the historiography of the West between the wars, however, his very singularity leaves behind a conundrum. The United States had become the richest country in the world; its graduate schools had become the best resourced, its professors the most favourably endowed.[125] Where were its new social historians promised in the braver days of 1912? The war plainly made some difference and Peter Novick's thesis of a collapsing ideal of objectivity comments on a substantial malaise. Perhaps more crushing was a sense of lost cultural optimism that had so readily fired the progressivism of the pre-war period. Rather than think concurrently of the French, perhaps one ought to recall the English and the Whig tradition that had at least as much to do with American historiography as anything happening in Berlin or Paris. Baxter Adams hung on a

---

125 When Becker went to Cornell in 1917 his interviewers felt unable to tell him what the requirements of the post might be. 'We have assumed', he was told, 'that whatever you found convenient and profitable to do would be sufficiently advantageous to the university and satisfactory to the students' (quoted in Smith 1956).

banner in his new seminar room at Hopkins the chant of Edward Freeman: 'All history is past politics and all politics present history.' Just as Freeman's liberalism left his successors unprepared for crisis in 1914, so Adams's found the various catastrophes of 1917 too confusing to accommodate and too dispiriting to challenge.

11

ANNALES: THE FRENCH SCHOOL

Thinking concurrently about the French remains a major imperative, despite the distance between Columbia and the Sorbonne. The need for doing so does not disappear in the absence of a manifest *Methodenstreit*, for the French had their own version; nor does the lack of a Pirenne or a Lamprecht in pre-war France provide a case for its marginality. As one looks forward into the period of European disaster between 1918 and 1939, the impression strengthens that the *belle époque* concealed a time of transition that would provide the groundwork for a series of developments that would make France the most exciting forum of historical thought between the great wars of the twentieth century. The date of fundamental importance within that period is one known to everyone who studies historiography at all: 1929, the year when Marc Bloch and Lucien Febvre founded a new periodical to which they, under pressure from their publisher, gave the title *Annales d'histoire économique et sociale*. Though the subtitle has changed, *Annales* has remained an avatar for one approach and become the name not only of a publication but also of a major school of historical enquiry, the most celebrated and admired, lamented and despised school of historiography to which the present century has given rise. Much of the resonance of *Annales*' foundation derives from the conditions of the inter-war period, as we shall see. But no small degree of influence attaches to developments within French historiography in those crucial years of

103

transition before 1914 that we have observed in the cases of Germany, Britain and the United States. *Annales* has a history *avant la lettre*.

How far back this fuller perspective requires one to reach depends on which characteristics seem most urgent in the range of tendencies that would eventually emerge in *Annales*. For an American observer such as Carlton Hayes, writing in 1920, the mood represented by Henri Berr (a figure often taken to be an inspiration for the thinking of Bloch and Febvre) appeared as anti-*belle époque* as Lytton Strachey's recent *Eminent Victorians* had been anti-Victorian. Hayes juxtaposed Berr's views with the ones he associated with Robinson's New History: 'their ideas represent[ed] a profound reaction on the part of the twentieth century against the narrow specialization of the nineteenth and the attempt to return to the interests of the eighteenth century.'[126] Set in a larger frame, on the other hand, those ideas have more of the nineteenth century in them than caught his eye. This is true, not only because challenges to existing orthodoxies contained in ventures such as Vidal de la Blache's *Annales de géographie* and Durkheim's *Année sociologique* began in the 1890s but, more importantly, because those challenges were posed to an orthodoxy that its critics badly misunderstood and caricatured. Out of their misunderstanding has grown a later one: that the mood of *Annales* came out of the rejection of traditional, often diplomatic, history symbolized by the profession's flagship journal, the *Revue historique*, which remained wedded to the approaches proclaimed by Langlois and Seignobos in their notorious manual of method published in 1898.[127] All effective cartoons contain something genuine, but this one stands in need of refinement.

---

126 Quoted in Siegel 1983. This volume of research papers (Carbonell and Livet (1983)), on which the present section draws heavily, offers much the best overview currently available of the condition of French historiography in the early twentieth century. It is a great pity that it is not more generally available outside the larger university collections that hold the 'Recherches et Documents' series of the Société Savante d'Alsace et des Regions de l'Est (*Tome* XXI). Meanwhile there is some relief from the appalling sycophancy attaching to the historiography of the *annalistes* in a recent critical study by Dosse 1987.

127 Langlois and Seignobos 1898. The lack of attention accorded these scholars under the influence of *annaliste* orthodoxies persists even in the most recent studies. It is arresting that so distinguished an historian as Peter Burke allows Seignobos, 'the symbol of everything the reformers opposed', a little more recognition than orthodoxy

Perhaps the influence and outlook of Gabriel Monod in his later career have been especially undervalued. Editor of the *Revue historique* until 1912, he presided over the empire that Berr and Febvre and Bloch sought to undermine; and certainly his acute sense of German source-criticism and relentless pursuit of a form of professionalization could be depicted as part of the target for radical social historians after 1900. Yet the historian of the *Revue*, Alain Corbin, finds Monod in retrospect 'complex, ambiguous, even perplexing': a man caught between his devotion to the tradition of Michelet and his admiration for what German scholarship had achieved in the nineteenth century (Corbin 1983: 106). Rather than oppose the synthesis of disciplines or the framing of hypotheses for historical testing – a crucial call among the young Turks – he believed in doing both, but *only* when the discipline had reached a point at which it had sufficient solidity in its professional practice to benefit from and exercise control over the thrust of radical initiatives. His Turks, moreover, were quite as young as those belonging to the opposition camp: the *Revue* was a product of overwhelmingly young historians rather than a vehicle for the elderly conservatives, as it is often implied to have been. Here he is in 1896 with his own criticisms of feeble approaches among historians and an agenda that Febvre himself could almost have written:

> On s'est trop habitué en histoire à s'attacher surtout aux manifestations brillantes, retantissantes ou éphémères de l'activité humaine, grands événements ou grands hommes, au lieu d'insister sur les grands et lents mouvements des institutions, des conditions économiques et sociales qui sont la partie vraiment intéressante de l'évolution humaine, celle qui peut être analysée avec quelque certitude et, dans une certaine mesure, ramenée à des lois.

> (quoted in Rebérioux 1983: 219–20)

Similar points could be made about Langlois and Seignobos. Certainly their approach to factuality would prove far too constraining for radical social historians, but the bulk of their insistence on accurate source-criticism and documentation, drawn from Seignobos's period in Germany in the 1870s, rather as Monod's had been acquired a decade earlier, would have struck Bloch, with his own German experience

---

permits while granting him insufficient attention to spell his name properly; Burke 1990: 10.

behind him, as unexceptionable. The point lay not in deriding documentary scholarship but in transcending it by extending the subject's comparative and disciplinary base.

Pressures in this direction came largely from outside the profession; and their effects insist that French historiography in the early twentieth century be conceived as a fragment from a more general intellectual history. The arrival of Paul Vidal de la Blache as a teacher at the *Ecole Normale Supérieure* in 1877 ensured, for example, that the teaming of geography with history would become a powerful and permanent feature of French undergraduate education, while his own *Annales de géographie*, appearing from 1891, gave those longing for a more research-grounded history a model of how to proceed. Instead of reading a landscape as the conditioner of a passive population – the thing that shapes them – Vidal insisted that the relationship was reciprocal at its weakest and that, argued in its stronger sense, a physical landscape should be viewed as having been formed by those who live in it so that the latter becomes an artefact bearing the picture of its creators, 'une médaille', as his resonant remark goes, 'frappée à l'image d'un peuple'. Only a small degree of exaggeration informed Febvre's recollection in 1953 that 'la géographie vidallienne' had engendered an approach that evolved into the *Annales* style of history (see Baker 1984: 5). If anything, the comment became more appropriate as time passed and especially following the appearance of Vidal's study of France in 1903. One sees the impression that this might have made on the young Marc Bloch whose degree at the *Ecole Normale* took the form of a dual-subject study of history and geography. By the time the first Congress of Historical Geography met at Brussels in 1930, those writers associated with the *Annales* impetus had been deploying geographical insights for a generation in their historical questions and research. 'It is somewhat absurd,' a leading historical geographer has conceded recently, 'that *annalistes* seem to have both learned and practised Paul de la Blache's principles of human geography more soundly and faithfully than have many French geographers' (Baker 1984: 2). Nor need one restrict the comment to geography: it seems hardly less relevant to refer to the sociology of Durkheim or Maurice Halbwachs, whom Bloch and Febvre encountered at Strasbourg after the war, or the anthropology of Marcel Mauss. Closer still to what became the *annaliste* home lay the development of specialist economic history with the first number in 1908 of the *Revue d'histoire économique et sociale*, a precursor in some ways of the *Economic History Review* (1927) and Luigi Einaudi's *Rivista di storia economica* (1936).[128]

That future *annalistes* should have sought to run rival disciplines together into a common cause owed little to chance associations. It followed the logic established by an academic mood of synthesis which no one enhanced more consistently than Henri Berr (1863–1954). Despite his enormous output, Berr never achieved the intellectual stardom of Bloch and Febvre, but his intellectual role in shifting historical enquiry in France was quite central. He was not an historian, primarily, but a philosopher whose doctoral thesis in the University of Paris had focused on the prospect of synthesizing historical knowledge in order to reverse the fragmentation of the subject that recent developments seemed to threaten.[129] The project ruined his career: he was rejected, together with Simiand, by the *Collège de France* in 1912 and his refusal to espouse any singular discipline left him marooned between all of them. But his *Revue de synthèse historique*, which began its appearance from the turn of the century, represents a remarkable monument to an original mind. It attracted, moreover, some of the brightest historians of their generation: we find Febvre writing for it by 1905, Bloch from 1912. And the alliances formed in these years carried through into the post-war era to become the basis for much new thinking in the Strasbourg period after 1919. A modern definition of the *Annales* movement – 'the attempt by French scholars to adapt economic, linguistic, sociological, geographical, anthropological, psychological, and natural science notions to the study of history and to infuse a historical orientation into the social and human sciences' (Stoianovich 1976: 19) – shows if nothing else the length of Berr's shadow.

We see it in his series 'L'Evolution de l'humanité', in which books by Febvre and Bloch would later appear, each with an enthusiastic introduction by Berr himself. Febvre was Bloch's senior by eight years.

---

128 For an account of these, see Allegra and Torre 1977: 276, 303.
129 'L'avenir de la philosophie: esquisse d'une synthèse de la connaissance de l'histoire' (Paris, 1898). In the published version he wrote of the need 'd'unifier l'histoire et la sociologie, les deux pôles de la même réalité, de l'individu et des institutions' (see Siegel 1983: 206).

He had come to Paris from Nancy, where his father taught, and spent a formative four years at the *Ecole Normale* astride the new century (1898–1902). His doctoral thesis on Philip II and the Franche-Comté (a district of south-eastern France close to the Swiss border) took many years to complete: he was 33 when the work finally emerged in 1911. Through Berr's journal he had already begun, however, both to manipulate some of his data and to think about method, so that the complete thesis contained some of the constituents of *annaliste* approaches. From there he moved towards writing one of his most important books, a *Geographical Introduction to History*. It appeared some years after the First World War and one thinks of it as an inter-war project; but he had put together some of the material and started writing before the war changed Febvre's perspective. It did so partly because he, like Bloch, served in the army. Febvre spent the war years in a machine-gun company and rose to the rank of captain. But the experience inevitably brought with it an anti-Teutonic backlash, perhaps the greater for Febvre's never having studied in Germany as had so many of his contemporaries. This came through in his analysis of the German nationalistic geographer Friedrich Ratzel (1844–1904) whose association of soil and people Febvre found disturbing in the light of the past four years; he countered with his plea for a human geography that drew on history for its explanations rather than race or *Vaterland*. The collaboration with Bloch in the University of Strasbourg began in 1920 and Febvre was intensely preoccupied with establishing the credibility of their method not only in the foundation of *Annales* in 1929 but in his explosive reviewing, which was prodigious, and his direction of research students. His best-known work, on Rabelais and the possibility of religious unbelief in the sixteenth century, did not appear until the middle of the Second World War (Febvre 1942).

So much is impressive about Febvre that one loses sight of what is not. A feeling sometimes creeps over the reader that Febvre's interest lies in a rather self-indulgent form of historical propaganda. The *Combats pour l'histoire* (1953) seem everywhere, leaving a nostalgia for forms of history that do not begin with combat. It is as though his mind would not turn unless he could find a straw figure to bayonet, which is why reviewing became a natural outlet. Even the major books have to be understood in this way. The bland title of his book about historical geography barely conceals the attack, of which it essentially consists, on German conceptions, with a balancing defence of Vidal's method enshrined in the *Tableau*, 'a unique book, with a character of its own, a masterpiece, but devoid of all dogmatism and quite inimitable' (Febvre 1925: 18). The study of Rabelais likewise takes the form of a reply to Abel Lefranc's account of him.[130] In affirming the unavailability of unbelief to a sixteenth-century writer Febvre made an intelligent, original point and opened a channel of enquiry that has been assiduously followed in post-war political theory. Whether it needed 450 pages to express it raises a different question. Indeed Febvre's discourse which, quite as much as his language, is implacably, untranslatably French, can provoke the fantasy that he may have taken a bet with someone to see how many pages he could write without stating a substantive historical proposition. For some historians the result approximates to playful wit: they applaud his innovative qualities, admire his lightness of touch (see e.g. Burke 1973). Readers outside his culture may none the less be forgiven for believing that there is too much of Febvre. They agree from Madrid to Oslo, whatever their nationality or historical orientation or poetic sensibility or sense of humour, that there is too little of Bloch.

More lies behind this recognition than Bloch's murder by the Nazis when he was 57. It rests on the character of his work, which left the rhetoric to his partner and concentrated on turning an ungovernable enthusiasm for knowing about past people into texts that almost seem over-silted out of a compulsion to demonstrate, elucidate, interrogate. There is a near-tangible aversion to posture and a level of commitment that pervades the text in its perpetual dialogue between contention and source. And each study feels like a report on work in progress, as though the future will change the past as a matter of course and require its constant rewriting. For that reason, the erasure of Bloch's personal future, known to the reader but not to the author, gives each text a special poignancy.

His Jewishness carries much of the imprint of that unknown future: one wonders whether, without it, he would not have seen out the war

---

130 Abel Lefranc had written a series of studies including *Le Visage de François Rabelais* (1925) and *L'Œuvre de Rabelais d'après les recherches les plus récentes* (1932). For a very different view of Febvre, see Bentley 1997, ch. 35.

in his library, like Febvre. In Lyon his father, Gustave Bloch, had become a distingished scholar as professor of ancient history and an expert on Roman Gaul; he returned to the *Ecole Normale* to teach almost immediately after Bloch's birth and the family moved to Paris. And to the extent that the younger Bloch also made his way to the *Ecole Normale*, there is an echo of Febvre's biography. From 1904 onwards their paths diverged. Bloch made geography part of his degree and, following his graduation in 1908, he spent a year in Germany – at Berlin and Leipzig, where he came across Lamprecht. His return to Paris and the *Fondation Thiers* between 1909 and 1912 helped lay his own foundation for much later research and gave rise to his study of the *Île de France* (1913), but his life, like Febvre's, was to undergo fundamental disruption: first in provincial schoolteaching but then through the war which affected him more, possibly, than most historians by teaching him how to look instead of read. Separated from his books, he found himself inserted into the countryside, albeit one scarred from perpetual shelling. He took to noticing field sizes and shapes; he listened to those soldiers from peasant backgrounds who knew the rhythms of rural life. A process of intense speculation about using landscape as a source has its origins, probably, in these years, between acts of conspicuous gallantry in the front line. Bloch realized the degree to which historians, because they are often so tied to documentation, begin at the earliest point of their story and look for relics that lead up to their point of interest. He came to believe that much could be done by reversing this procedure – starting with what exists now as a matter of certainty and then working backwards in the manner of the genealogist towards a less certain past. The point would not lie in making the past a vehicle for the present, in the style of British Whig history, but rather in seeing parts of it, usually aspects of physical geography, as a reliable and unused source from which to extrapolate bygone structures of landowning and settlement.

None of this bore fruit immediately. Teaching and participation in the work of a new department preoccupied him after his appointment in 1919 to the chair of medieval history at the new University of Strasbourg. His contact with the Febvrian inferno, as well as with those working in parallel fields such as the sociologist Maurice Halbwachs, generated an intense and self-conscious historiographical radicalism which had its first expression in *Les Rois thaumaturges* (1924), a study of the environment and *mentalité* which gave rise to 'the king's touch' as a healing device. But the commitment to building up a knowledge of the patchwork-quilt of rural society and to seeing the whole within a comparative perspective, such as Pirenne urged at Brussels in 1923, carried on at the quieter level of note and docket. Some of the printed regional material he plainly read at home; there were days, too, in the archives in Paris, producing material for the bottom drawer. Without his summons from Oslo, he always said, the book would probably have remained a mental patchwork. Certainly it was an invitation from the *Institut pour l'Etude Comparative des Civilisations* for a course of lectures to be delivered in the Norwegian capital in the autumn of 1929 that compelled the conversion of intimation to text. For all its tone of pre-emptive apology, the book that would emerge under a clumsy and prosaic title – *Les Caractères originaux de l'histoire rurale française* (1931) – shows better than any other the calibre of Bloch's thought and his originality of vision over what he believed the subject to be about. Together with the better-known two volumes of *La Société féodale* (1939–40), it gives an indication of what the *Annales* tendency might have become had he lived.

What remains striking about Bloch's historical thinking in the 1930s is its commitment to the analysis of change over long periods and the search for structures which would make temporal and geographical variety reducible to intelligible patterns. *Les Caractères* had both dimensions: it surveyed the chronology from the early medieval *seigneurie* to the agricultural revolution of the eighteenth century; and it proposed ideal types of 'agrarian regimes' which reduced the complexity of French rural experience to three forms of field-shape intersected by two types of plough, the *araire* or scratch-plough of the south and the wheeled *charrue* of the north. There are Durkheimian flourishes. In the middle of a structural meditation in the chapter on 'Agrarian Life' one can meet a one-sentence paragraph arranged as a *pensée*: 'As in the regions of open fields, these material manifestations [enclosures] were the outward expression of underlying social realities' (Bloch [1931] 1966: 57). Later, in the less-remarked section called 'Social Groupings', the stirrings of a possible social history of medieval civilization occasionally come to the surface. 'To sum up' (his detailed discussion of the *manse*), it seems that a number of weighty if slightly mysterious happenings lie behind the superficially trivial fact that in the eleventh century estate surveys are arranged by *manses*, in the thirteenth or seventeenth centuries by fields or households: the reduction of the family to a narrower and more changeable compass, the total disappearance of public taxation, and a radical transformation in the internal organization of the *seigneurie* must all have played their part.

(ibid. 163)

Ideas of this kind were developed in a systematic way in the two volumes of *Feudal Society*. Bloch concerned himself with an entire civilization: its economic structures, its social stratification, its sources of power. He saw a division within it by period. The earlier had a character determined by insecurity in the wake of Islamic and Scandinavian threats. Because no unified social structure could congeal in such circumstances, ties of local dependency became common, marked by military obligation operating as a *quid pro quo* for protection: the crucial background to the development of 'feudalism'.[131] In the later period particular cultural and technological developments conflicted with the original *raison d'être* of the social system; but that system had established itself in so profound a way that only certain forms of adaptation could remain possible – a key to how feudalism became a sclerotic way of organizing social and military resources.[132] Like Pirenne's understanding of the development of medieval trade, the image perhaps suffered from too sharp a resolution; but that must always happen to innovative conceptualization and Bloch always knew that it did.

By the time Bloch's volumes appeared, he had finally succeeded in making the move back to Paris. Since 1936 he had held the chair of economic history at the Sorbonne: truant had turned prefect. The new journal had meanwhile dominated much of the research time of both Febvre and Bloch in its early years. They imposed on it a tone calculated to *épater les bourgeois*, especially bourgeois professors. They invited scholars from all over Europe and America to contribute,

---

131 For a penetrating modern critique of these assumptions, see Reynolds 1994, esp. ch. 3.

132 I follow here Daniel Chirot's characterization of Bloch's argument: see Chirot 1984: esp. pp. 24–5.

especially where they could write on subjects that joined together past and present in the way that the Strasbourg mood deemed appropriate. In practice this meant that *Annales* soon lost its ancient and medieval contributions and became more securely located in the period since 1500.[133] Differences of approach between the editors made themselves felt. Febvre wanted to use *Annales* as a weapon against the establishment, deploying radical contemporary history with a minimum of academic apparatus; Bloch had more interest in printing imaginative history of all kinds. Febvre's move to the *Collège de France* in 1933 made communication that much harder to sustain and by the time of Pirenne's death in 1935 fissures had appeared that threatened the future of the enterprise. Bloch's famous piece examining the history of the watermill began life as one attempt to resuscitate *Annales*; and it was during the 'second wave' of the journal's life that he and Febvre attempted a definition of *annaliste* method. Seen against the background of the previous fifty years, it seems not so very different from what Monod had tried to achieve, though the surface-texture has a Febvrian choppiness:

> Préoccupation du general, goût de l'histoire totalitaire, scrutée par alliance entre les disciplines; refus de soumettre aux routines alternées d'une historiographie oratoire et d'une érudition sans horizon; décisions très fermes de n'attaquer le sujet qu'après avoir tout d'abord dressé un questionnaire assez serré pour que rien d'important ne risque de glisser entre ses mailles, assez simple pour s'adapter, chemin faisant, aux révélations de l'enquête elle-même; dans l'établissement de ce premier schema comme dans le choix des instruments d'investigation ou d'expression – cartes ou statistiques par exemple – le sense le plus juste à la fois de la réalité concrète et des phénomènes de profondeur: si vraiment ces traits composent la méthode des 'Annales'.[134]

---

133 Carole Fink has a helpful chapter, on which I have drawn, analysing the content of *Annales* in her biography of Marc Bloch, Fink 1989: 128–65.

134 Editorial statement in 1937, quoted in Allegra and Torre 1977: 303–4. 'A preoccupation with the general, a taste for global history examined in an inter-disciplinary way; a refusal to stumble into the twin pitfalls of a rhetorical historiography on the one hand or pointless demonstrations of erudition on the other; very firm decisions never to approach the subject until one has first asked questions which are both sufficiently precise as to avoid allowing anything of importance to slip through the net, but also flexible enough to be adjusted as one goes along in response to what the investigation throws up; a refined sense both of concrete reality but also of deeper, less visible

But, as Alain Corbin (1983: 109–10) rightly reminds a generation that may have become over-fascinated by *Annales*, this mood should be seen as only one part of a more general 'turn' in the intellectual direction of the 1930s – a mood that included in France the Marxist critiques of Mathiez,[135] Lefebvre,[136] Simiand[137] and others, and an anthropological surge associated among French thinkers preponderantly with the writing of Marcel Mauss.[138]

The ascendancy gained by *Annales* historians in the post-war years when Braudel became their wayward guru masks just how fragile the project seemed during those first ten years. There were times when Febvre, in particular, felt like throwing in the towel; times when publication dates passed with the copy not ready (Fink 1989: 144, 149).

---

phenomena when drawing up the plan of action and its various tools – maps or statistics, for example: truly, these are the characteristics which inform the method of the *"Annales"*.' On the watermill piece and the importance of Bloch's revisions of early positions through the 1930s, see Davies 1967.

135 Albert Mathiez (1874–1932). Socialist from a peasant family in Franche-Comté. Taught by Monod and supervised by Alphonse Aulard, of whom he became a life-long critic. Member of the Communist Party for three years (1920–3). Main appointments Besançon (1911–19) and Dijon (1919–26). Achieved lectureship at Paris but a stroke terminated his career. Main field French Revolution and especially Robespierre: *La Revolution Française* (1922–7); *La Reaction thermidorienne* (1929); *Le Directoire* (1934).

136 Georges Lefebvre (1874–1959). Flemish: father a bookkeeper. Taught by Petit-Dutaillis at Lille. Schoolteacher before and during war. Marxist from mid-1930s. Chair in history of the French Revolution at the Sorbonne (1937). Concentration on what he called 'L'influence intermentale' during the years of revolutionary upheaval and anxiety. See *Les Paysans du Nord pendant la Revolution française* (1924); *La Grande Peur de 1789* (1932); *Foules historiques* (1934); *Les Thermidoriens* (1937).

137 François Simiand (1873–1935). Economic historian who read philosophy at *Ecole Normale*; influenced by Durkheim and Lévy-Bruhl. Socialist voicing admiration for Jaurès and Blum; friend of Péguy and Daniel Halévy (younger brother of Elie). Ran a socialist publishing company and then became librarian at the new Ministry of Labour (1906). Preoccupation historically with workers' wages. From 1910 lectured on history of economic theory at *Ecole Pratique des Hautes Etudes*; head of history department by 1924. Central work: *Le Salaire: l'évolution sociale et la monnaie* (1932).

138 Marcel Mauss (1872–1950). Durkheim's nephew. Possibly under his influence rejected religion of Jewish parents. Avid Dreyfusard. One of the pre-eminent ethnographers of his generation; chairs at *Ecole Pratique* (until 1930) and then *Collège de France* (1931–9). His early work on magic may have contributed to Durkheim's view of the sociology of religion. Classic study of *Le Don* (1925), a transcultural account of gifts and their function.

The more telling threat came, for all that, from outside academia. During the middle years of the decade *Annales* began, in its zest for contemporary history, to run articles on Nazism. By the spring of 1939 it became apparent to those with a finger on the political pulse that scholarship was about to be overtaken by events. Certainly none of their implications were lost on Bloch who, as a Jew and a former soldier, felt an overwhelming sense of concern and duty. The young Braudel, safe in the University of São Paulo, came home to enlist and spent much of the war in a prison camp as a consequence. For each of the 'Big Three' the years after 1939 proved momentous. Febvre's survival placed him at the forefront of the new *Sixième Section* and allowed him guidance of the journal whose new title he inaugurated: *Annales: économies, sociétés, civilisations*. Bloch's promise ended among a group of fellow members of the Resistance in a spatter of machine-gun fire in a field outside Lyon on 16 June 1944. Braudel took with him into German captivity a collection of ideas for a book about the history of the Mediterranean Sea. He emerged, famously, with a manuscript which was to provide him with a doctorate and a chair at the *Collège de France* within five years. When we look back over the historiography of twentieth-century France, as of Germany or Russia or Italy or Spain, these events remind us of the centrality of military forces in their shaping, which were quite as important as intellectual ones, and recall the frequent presence of ideological repressions and threats far beyond the imagination of the despised professors of the Sorbonne.

12

REPRESSION AND EXILE

So consuming and notorious was the repression of historical scholarship by agents of the Third Reich that we readily overlook earlier evidence of intellectual control by other states seeking to starve curiosity as a means of leaving awkward questions unanswered. Take the case of Russia. Long before the rise of Bolshevism as a major force, the destabilization of tsarist society left some sensitive Moscow intellectuals reflecting whether they could remain in the country as the interference of the authorities increased over curricula and public attitudes in the universities. One such – perhaps in a sense the first émigré historian of the twentieth century – was Paul Vinogradoff. He had known about Europe's attractions for many years for his original subject had turned on the nature and significance of English villeinage.[139] A pupil of Mommsen's in Berlin in the late 1870s, he went on to make the acquaintance of the formidable British legal and constitutional historian Frederic Maitland when he worked on British material in the Public Record Office in 1883. But only in 1901 did he make the decision to leave Russia for good and it was during his tenure

---

139 *Villainage* [sic] *in England* (1892) was followed by *The Growth of the Manor* (1905). For a collection of papers examining the entire relationship indicated here, see Kozicki 1993.

of the chair of jurisprudence at Oxford that he acted in turn as an influential teacher, bridging the divide between the generation of Mommsen and that of highly significant medievalists such as Frank Stenton and Helen Cam.[140] M. I. Rostovtzeff came closer to their generation than to Vinogradoff's: he had been born near Kiev in 1870. His peregrinations round Europe came in the 1890s; the decision to go he delayed until after the 1917 Revolution. In his case the emigration led from St Petersburg to the Sterling Chair of Ancient History at Yale by way of Oxford and Madison, Wisconsin. In his case, moreover, the relationship between his experience and how he conceived the past in his historical writing became more demonstrable than in that of Vinogradoff. His determination that civilization should win and barbarism, defined to look very like Bolshevik ideals, should fail, informed and energized his earlier works, especially the *Social and Economic History of the Roman Empire* (also Rostovtzeff 1926–7; 1941; cf. Wes 1990).

Much the same deployment of experience as a touchstone for historical interpretation lies embedded in the work of one of the most serious historical thinkers of the century, a Polish-Russian who was sent to England for his education in order to avoid the threat of further Russian oppression in the region of Galicia. One wonders what sort of figure Lewis Bernstein Namier would have cut had he remained in his own country, because it seems overwhelmingly clear that his year at the London School of Economics, where he was impressed by the geopolitical perspectives of Halford Mackinder, and then the stimulus

---

140 Frank Merry Stenton (1880–1967) spent most of his academic life at University College, Reading, until it became a university in 1926. He was professor of modern history there from 1912 until 1946 when he became vice-chancellor for the four years before he retired in 1950. The seminal works are *The First Century of English Feudalism 1066–1166* (1932) and *Anglo-Saxon England* (1943). Helen Maud Cam (1885–1968) spent the early part of her career at Royal Holloway College, London, where she had been an undergraduate, apart from a year at Bryn Mawr. But she spent the period from 1921 to 1948 at Girton College, Cambridge, before taking a chair at Harvard for the last six years preceding her retirement in 1954. Most of her output is to be found in articles and essays, collected in *Liberties and Communities in Medieval England: Case Studies in Administration and Topography* (1944) and *Law Finders and Law Makers in Medieval England* (1962). She became a Fellow of the British Academy in 1945 and was the first woman to deliver the Raleigh Lecture.

of Balliol College, Oxford, where he came into contact with the mind of Arnold Toynbee, played a critical role in fathering the man. And the migration to England, once achieved, would never be reversed. First in Oxford but then, after a period in business in the United States, in Manchester where he became professor of modern history, Namier brought to the study of both British and recent European history a formidable forensic intelligence which he used to celebrate the past of Britain's elites and the future of Europe's Jews, seeing, like Rostovtzeff, a fragility in civilization which barbarism would always threaten and, like so many Jewish intellectuals of the twentieth century, suspecting a predisposition in European society to marginalize and victimize Jews. The first theme came out strongly in the early work on eighteenth-century politics, which Namier so powerfully reoriented that he gave the language a new verb: to Namierize. His method turned on a severe reliance on the scrutiny of individuals as central historical actors and the power of individual biography to explain events without recourse to sociological or ideological structures. *The Structure of Politics at the Accession of George III* (1929) showed that explanatory structures in the eighteenth century could be identified but they had to be understood at an atomized level of individual agents and families, not as an engagement between Whig and Tory principles in which he largely disbelieved and announced that his protagonists did also. His second thrust appeared in his studies of Europe in the age of the dictators, especially *Europe in Decay* (1950) and *In the Nazi Era* (1951). For all his lifelong attachment to 'English' values, his émigré status never quite left him and certainly never left his sense of which historical problems ought to be studied (see J. Namier 1971; Rose 1980; Colley 1989).

It follows that a sophisticated sense of the period should resist an instinct that fascism and Nazism supplied the only vehicles for intellectual repression and resettlement in this most repressive of periods. They nevertheless do supply contexts of spectacular importance in explaining why the historiographies of Italy and Germany developed (or failed to develop) as they did; and they give luminous examples of displaced persons who would take their historical talents away from central Europe and towards Britain or – especially in the case of displaced Germans – towards the United States, with significant consequences for the enrichment of two cultures and the impoverishment of several others.[141] Detailed treatments of the Italian and German cases appear in Chapters 21 and 22 of Bentley 1997 and we need not reconnoitre ground that is covered here. Yet in thinking about the global weight that we need to accord the phenomenon of displacement, certain points occur naturally here.

One of them is a thought about generations. Not only did mature, working historians find their lives uprooted by circumstances beyond all prediction and control, but they took with them into exile their children, some of whom would in turn emerge as major historians in their own right but as persons who now had an entirely different identity: people who might have taken into adult life only a shadowy recollection of the Soviet Revolution or of fascist politics in the 1930s but whose entire perspective would nevertheless be dominated by the experience. The Russian future Byzantinist, George Ostrogorski, was still in his teens when his family left St Petersburg. But the trajectory through Germany, where Percy Schramm taught him at Heidelberg, and Paris, where he met the influential Byzantinist Charles Diehl, propelled him in the direction of Yugoslavia and his chair at Belgrade after 1933. For British medievalists, by the same token, Michael Postan seemed an emblem of the Soviet Revolution which had driven his family away but whose prehistory nevertheless left in Postan a permanent concern with the medieval economy, issues of trade and social structure which would lead him to a chair in economic history at Cambridge, and a hardly less significant marriage to the distinguished medievalist Eileen Power.[142] For relics of fascist and Nazi displacement, think only of two major historical personalities of the years after the Second World War, G. R. Elton and Franco Venturi. The first we associate with Cambridge and the Tudors, the second with a number of Italian universities and the Enlightenment in Italy in the eighteenth century.[143] Yet the story of each has a common thread wound around

---

141 The phenomenon of intellectual exile has given rise to a substantial literature of which that treating Europe's historians should be seen as a complement. Some examples of the wider lens include Lixl-Purcell 1988; Tucker 1991; Krohn 1993.

142 Her life has recently been assessed by the economic historian, Maxine Berg (1996).

143 G. R. Elton (1921–94) wrote a very large collection of books and papers. The latter he assembled as *Studies in Tudor and Stuart Politics* (1974–84). Among the more

the history of Mussolini and Hitler. Venturi's father was an art historian who took his son into exile with him in 1931; so the teenager's environment shifted from Rome to Paris. The removal did not prevent his internment during the war but doubtless coloured his view of a special Italian past characterized by the best elements of the Enlightenment, a repeated concern in the volumes of his series on the *Settecento riformatore* and elsewhere in an impressive body of writing. 'Elton' was an English invention imposed by the army to prevent confusion over his real name – Ehrenburg – and became an alternative identity which masked the background in Prague until excitement or relaxation revived his trilled 'R's. The Ehrenburgs had left Czechoslovakia under threat of Nazi occupation and thus precipitated Elton's future sense of himself as an adoptive Englishman who believed that continentals had too much awareness of the past for their own good and who preferred the cooler perspectives of British empiricism and national forget-fulness.

A second point also concerns geography. Entire sections of continental Europe lost their Jews in the black smoke of Himmler's vision. But some did not; and for students of intellectual history, within which Jewish historians have always played a particular part, a radical disjunction becomes apparent in post-war Europe. It has been well observed by a historian of the *Annales*, for example, that the role of Jewish scholars in giving that persuasion a strong cosmopolitan, anti-nationalist flavour should be seen as an element in its post-war complexion, for all the tragedy of Bloch's murder.[144] Equally, one can argue that the systematic snuffing-out of Jewish brilliance in Germany and Austria has brought about a long-term, possibly permanent dead-ening of the intellectual cultures once supported in those countries. Perhaps the impact on social theory and philosophy comes most

---

significant work on British history one might mention *England under the Tudors* (3rd edn, 1991); *The Tudor Constitution* (2nd edn, 1982); *Policy and Police* (1972); *The Parliament of England* 1559–1581 (1986). Franco Venturi (b.1914) has been likewise prolific, with an interesting division of interest between Italy and Russia and an impressive range of languages: *Il populismo russo* (1952); *Utopia and Reform in the Enlightenment* (1971); *Italy and the Enlightenment* (1972); *Les intellectuels, le people* (1977); *Venezia nel secondo settecento* (1980); *Giovinezza di Diderot* (1713–53) (1988).

144 Stoianovich 1976. He notes, however, that the *annalistes* have never made Jewish studies, or any form of ethno-history, central to their outlook (ibid. 51–6).

quickly to mind in the repression of the Frankfurt and Vienna schools of thought – an impact not lost on history because many of the more penetrating questions available to inter-war historians had their origins in critical social thought.[145] Thus a Karl Popper might be projected from Vienna and end up, via New Zealand in his case, in the London School of Economics. But the lesson is equally valid for historians. The distance from Vienna to Rome reduced, as a result of policies associated with Hitler and Mussolini, to the few hundred yards between the London School of Economics and University College, London, when that College accepted Arnaldo Momigliano as professor of ancient history in 1951. Few careers better make the point. The greatest historiographer of the twentieth century was an Italian Jew who had been a pupil of Gaetano de Sanctis at Turin and was deprived of his chair in Rome by Mussolini's race laws. Brief stays in Oxford and Bristol prefaced Momigliano's tenure of a post in which he was to produce the volumes of *Contributi* which have become the greatest landmark of classical and antique learning witnessed since the Second World War.[146] London had no more right to Momigliano than to Popper; it benefited immeasurably from both.

Where this notion of a global redrawing of mental maps makes itself overwhelmingly felt is in the diaspora of Jews from Nazi Germany itself after 1933 and in particular the common destination of so many of them. Immigration restrictions in Britain and possibly a discomfort about British culture felt by German intellectuals after their humiliation in 1918 helped them contemplate a bolder uprooting whose effect would be radical and often permanent. For someone like Wilhelm Levison, who worked on English and European history in the early medieval period, America seemed too great a wrench when the tightening of the racial laws in Germany forced him from his chair in Bonn. The University of Durham had given him an honorary degree,

---

145 For the Frankfurt School, see Wolin 1992; Wiggerhaus 1994. Much has been written on the Vienna circle, e.g. Coffa 1991; Menger 1994.
146 *Contributi alla storia degli studi classici (e del mondo antico)* (9 vols, Rome, 1955–92). Momigliano (1908–87) can be approached in English through his *Studies in Historiography* (1966) and his *Essays in Ancient and Modern Historiography* (1977), though they barely touch the surface of an output of more than 1,000 titles. Commemorative volumes include Weinberg 1988; Steinberg 1988; Dionisotto 1989.

doubtless under the recommendation of his friend, Bertram Colgrave, some years before; it took him in when he arrived in England in 1939 and he stayed there till his death in 1947, delivering his highly regarded Ford Lectures on England and the Continent in the eighth century in 1942.[147] Yet for many others America presented the more attractive alternative and the westward shift of Jewish historians from Germany seems in retrospect one of the more significant intellectual migrations of the twentieth century that now attracts serious scholarly attention.[148]

To an uncanny degree, many of them had originally been, or had turned into, pupils of Friedrich Meinecke. He shared the disillusion with Weimar felt by former nationalists but his pluralism and humanity led him to help colleagues in trouble as easily as it led to his sacking from the editorship of the *Historische Zeitschrift* by the Nazis. One should not over-press Meinecke's liberality: his preoccupation with the history of ideas had a Prussian twist and amounted to a metaphysical and sometimes mystical notion of the state as the outcome of moral endeavour. He placed the needs of the state on a supra-ethical plane, particularly in his study of *raison d'état* (Meinecke 1924). His pupils reflected his period and his leanings and they constituted a formidable group of émigrés, from Dietrich Gerhard (b.1896) to Felix Gilbert (b.1905), by way of Hans Baron, Hajo Holborn, Eckhart Kehr, Gerhard Masur and Hans Rosenberg.[149] The effect on American research and teaching in the modern history of Europe turned out to be prodigious and corrected, through the most painful of mechanisms, a serious imbalance left by the more inward-looking generation headed by Turner. And once the movement had begun, it did not halt with the end of hostilities in 1945. The post-war period saw a continued influx that raised the world-profile of American expertise (see Novick 1988: 378).

The concern with ideas emerges also from two of the most prominent medievalists driven from Berlin by the Nazis, not from the university lectures and seminars of Meinecke in their cases but from

---

147 The lectures were published after the war: see Levison 1946.
148 See in particular the very helpful volume of essays produced by the German Historical Institute in Washington: Lehmann and Sheehan 1991.
149 See Wolfgang Mommsen's superb portrait of 'Historiography in the Weimar Republic' in Lehman and Sheehan 1991, esp. 52ff.

the *Monumenta Germaniae Historica* when it was still housed there. In Ernst Kantorowicz and Theodor 'Ted' Mommsen, Germany lost two of its more famous historical names: the first because his strange, romantic, atavistic and (far worse in Berlin) unfootnoted life of Frederick II (1927) had given rise to waves of abuse and enthusiasm; the second because no grandson of the great ancient historian could have escaped fame, even if he had not been Max Weber's nephew. An ability in the one to think freshly through the problems of myth and symbol in modern thought, in the other to present small-scale essays investigating specific contexts in the intellectual history of the Middle Ages were lost to the German universities as they departed, in the case of Kantorowicz for the Institute for Advanced Study in Princeton (eventually) and for Princeton and Cornell in the case of Mommsen.[150] Kantorowicz had the greater intellect and his work had an innovative quality that would have made him comfortable among the future *annalistes* of Strasbourg. Indeed *The King's Two Bodies* (1957) could be placed on the same shelf as Marc Bloch's *Les Rois thaumaturges*, though it attempted a very different project. Kantorowicz had become pre-occupied by the dual status of medieval kings: as owners of a human body with an ordinary existence but also as custodians of a body politic with a constitutional, social and sometimes mystical existence. The first could suffer, sin and die; the second drew its sustenance from without, enjoyed various forms of immaculacy and could not arrange its own death. His section on 'The Crown as Fiction' travels quite as far in its imaginative drive as anything projecting from Braudellian Paris (see Kantorowicz 1957: 336–83).

Most of these émigrés did not develop new genres: they wrote in a familiar frame of post-Lamprechtian *Kulturgeschichte* or persisted in that Rankian emphasis on foreign policy and international relations that is reflected in a phrase such as *der Primat der Aussenpolitik*. The work of perhaps the best-known of the established émigrés, Hans Rothfels, may be taken as symptomatic of the group as a whole.[151] Sometimes, however, the task of one of these expatriates might include acting as a

---

150 Their intertwined careers are helpfully reviewed by Robert Lerner in Lehmann and Sheehan 1991: 188–205. For Kantorowicz, see Boureau 1990.

151 Hans Rothfels's *œuvre* significantly includes a book on the German resistance (*Die deutsche Opposition gegen Hitler* (1949), but its previous emphasis is in the Meineckian

mediator in presenting to a transatlantic audience the more adventurous ideas of one who stayed. Otto Hintze was to remain largely unknown except among specialists working on the Hohenzollern until Felix Gilbert edited his shorter pieces in the mid-1970s (Gilbert 1975; cf. Simon 1968). His lack of self-advertisement, which often came across as icy superiority, had doubtless contributed to the isolation and sadness of this lapsed *Weltpolitiker*; but we readily forget that he had resigned his chair in Berlin rather than submit to the racial inquisitions of the Nazis and died in lonely and miserable obscurity in 1940. Hintze's case underlines the point that staying in Germany should not be read as a form of collaboration: much depended on situation, temperament and stage of life, as well as political conviction or racial background. These latter characteristics could, of course, make remaining a sheer impossibility. One thinks of the difficulties of Veit Valentin, whose outspoken defence of liberal values under the Weimar Republic prevented him from achieving a post worthy of his scholarship and brought about his dismissal even from that, once the Nazis came to power.[152] Or one might recall the clouds gathering over the Warburg Institute in Hamburg by 1933.

Warburg's story pulls together a number of themes from these years of mounting anxiety for Jews.[153] As a member of a distinguished Jewish banking family, Aby Warburg (1866–1929) never had to worry about money. His passions were different: he adored art and collected books, financed by the family. He did so in order to pursue his own studies in art history, which resulted in many papers on the Renaissance and the impact on it, in particular, of classical modes of thought. There was

---

tradition of state and diplomatic history: *Carl von Clausewitz* (1920); *Bismarcks englische Bündnispolitik* (1924); *Bismarck und der Osten* (1934); *Ostraum, Preussentum und Reichsgedanke* (1935).

152 He had been sacked at Freiburg for holding incorrect views about German foreign policy and Tirpitz. For Valentin's subsequent problems, see Mommsen in Lehman and Sheehan 1991: 44–7: 'His fate as a determined democratic liberal, who in spite of respectable research achievements was never considered acceptable by official academic historiography, was in many ways representative of the trends prevailing in the German historical profession in the 1920s and 1930s.'

153 For the history of Warburg and his institute, see Ernst Gombrich's seminal account *Aby Warburg: an Intellectual Biography* (1970), which also contains an account of the library's migration by Warburg's assistant, Fritz Saxl.

a book on Botticelli. But the library that Warburg began to amass in his house in Hamburg began to take on a life of its own, not merely because of its size – there were much larger private libraries – but because its concentration on cultural history in the Burckhardtian sense and its relationship with Warburg's own intellectual priorities gave it a special coherence and utility for historians of art and Renaissance culture. Scholars would come to the house and try to make sense of the Byzantine cataloguing system invented by Warburg himself. By the 1920s the reputation of the collection had become so widespread that the ambitions of Warburg and his assistants turned towards the establishment of a major institute which could contain the books and offer civilized surroundings for visiting historians. Unfortunately these years also saw Warburg's obsession, for only an obsessive could have driven the collection forward, turning to neurosis; he became confined in a hospital for the mentally ill. He made a partial recovery – sufficient for him to see the inauguration of his dream of an Institute, under the aegis of the University of Hamburg, in 1924 and the move of the library into an adjacent and larger space in 1925. The death of Warburg in 1929 did not, therefore, destroy what he had made, for it had a financial and institutional framework that would permit the Institute's work to continue and expand. Far more crippling was the coming of the depression, which subverted the Warburg family's wealth, and then the arrival of the Nazis in power at the beginning of 1933. The 'solution' turned out to be an English one. Underpinned by Samuel Courtauld and the American wing of the Warburg family, the Warburg Institute transformed itself into a pile of boxes and moved to London in 1933; it was incorporated in the University of London during the Second World War. In this way the deranged new powers of Nazism cost Germany a new kind of history together with the prestige of the Institute and the journal that it launched in 1937. With the Institute went people, moreover, and the talents in particular of two young art historians, Erwin Panofsky and Ernst Gombrich, the latter of whom still, at the time of writing (1996), has a room at the Warburg Institute and whose vestigial Viennese accent still makes its mark on public radio.[154]

---

154 For Panofsky (1892–1968), see in particular his *Meaning in the Visual Arts* (1970)

Mapping these many moves in the age of communism, fascism and Nazism produces false impressions as well as necessary and important ones. For every historian obliged to seek refuge from repression, many more sat it out, kept their heads down and continued working amid difficult and uncertain circumstances. Nor should the historiography of the period come into focus as one dominated by responses to extreme doctrines. Seen in the round, the historical writing of the period between 1919 and 1945 seems as much conservative as radical; and when it *does* seem radical it often appears so in countries that were not repressive: the France of Febvre and Bloch, the America of Becker and Beard. Even within free societies, innovative thinking easily masks the face of traditional scholarship. Febvre comes to mind before Ferdinand Lot (1866–1952). Yet Lot's books (close to forty of them) and his persistent presence at the Sorbonne from 1909 to the beginning of the Second World War may eventually prove a greater influence on the historiography of the twenty-first century than anything Febvre said. Lot certainly thought so. Alphonse Aulard may have lacked the divine spark of a Bloch; but he reached the top sooner and stayed there longer. The Britain that nursed the radical futures of Christopher Hill, Eric Hobsbawm (himself a refugee from Berlin), Rodney Hilton and Edward Thompson also nursed the present of Bruce Macfarlane's Oxford and G. M. Trevelyan's Cambridge (see Cannadine 1993), neither of which threatened revolution. Yet the immediate future seemed to confirm that the torch had passed to a generation for whom the desperate realities of inter-war life played a major role. Few of those displaced went back. One finds occasional exceptions, such as the determined anti-fascist Salvemini[155] who had been driven out of Italy and had campaigned against Mussolini from America. He returned to his chair in Florence after the war when he was long past the age of retirement. But such stories are few. The centre of gravity in historical thought and writing had shifted not for one decade but for several.

---

and the account by M. A. Holly of *Panofsky and the Foundation of Art History* (1984). Gombrich's wide-ranging publications can be scrutinized in and supplemented by Onians 1994.

155 Gaetano Salvemini (1873–1957) had been professor of modern history at Florence between 1916 and his expulsion by the fascist government in 1925. He was eventually awarded a chair at Harvard (1934), but returned to Florence in 1949 at the age of 76.

13

POST-WAR MOODS

The resolution of the Second World War presents itself to memory in the 1990s as both an end and a beginning for some forms of historical writing. Some historians would go further and assert that 1945 is now the wrong place to start, inviting as it does the picture of a century riven in its centre when perhaps, even in German history, the continuities between the world of the 1930s and that of (say) the 1960s appear more compelling thirty years on than the sharp disjunctions of *die deutsche Katastrophe*.[156] At one level of logic, continuity can always be proved, of course: no one – not even if he or she suffered exile or persecution – could disown a personal past and all the conditioning elements associated with it. Yet there seems little doubt that historiography after 1950 did go in new directions in order to fit itself to a different world order and a series of intellectual and political shifts. To describe all the significant changes that have taken place since then would not only fill a brief introduction of this kind but require detailed examination of topics reviewed in the later chapters of Bentley 1997. And the long-term perspective needed for a successful reivew is not yet

---

156 For the continuity thesis, see an excellent collection of essays, Lehmann and Van Horn Melton 1994. *Die deutsche Katastrophe* (1946) was the title of Friedrich Meinecke's seminal attempt after the war to make sense of the Nazi past in a longer view of German historiography.

available: we are too much the product of the events and moods that we seek to analyse. An opportunity should be taken none the less to indicate some broad lines of development across the chronology and to catch up with some styles of historiography not treated in depth in this volume.

Because the Second World War and its global aftermath embraced hardly less than the world and because it therefore threw into historical awareness the cultures of Japan, Australasia, Russia and the United States as well as those of Europe, the fortunes of world history as a form of enquiry became fashionable again after 1945. The so-called Cold War between the United Sates and Soviet Russia and the Maoist revolution in China, with the Korean War to follow, helped assert a view of history that made conventional approaches to international history seem dated and lop-sided. Only a view of world history, rather than the study of relations between two or three states within the system, seemed to have scale enough to cope with these new perspectives and to underline the degree to which everyone was now living in a different world. Few historians felt the weight of this thought so severely as the British historian Geoffrey Barraclough, who by 1956 had come to see the historiography of Europe as so provincial that

> it would not be difficult to argue that we should be better off if we could scrap our histories of Europe and free our minds from their myopic concentration on the West. For such history, while it may conceivably serve to harden our prejudices and fortify us in our belief in the superiority of our traditions and values, is liable to mislead us dangerously about the actual distribution of power and the forces actually operative in the world in which we live. Moreover it inculcates a false sense of continuity, against which experience rebels, and obscures the fact that we are living in a world totally different, in almost all its basic preconditions, from that which Bismarck bestrode. . . . The questions we have to ask today have changed; and the past we look back upon from the small, surviving rock which still protrudes from the upheaval is totally different from the smooth expanse we saw stretching behind us before 1939.
>
> ('The Larger View of History', *Times Literary Supplement*, 6 January 1956)

Ten years later one American historian could regret that the number of books directed at world history was probably still smaller than the volume of works dealing with (say) seventeenth-century England (Erwin 1966; 1189).

These irritations were real enough; but the comments belie the degree to which subterranean movement had already begun. Two multi-volume works designed to reassess world perspectives had already appeared. One of them was French – the *Histoire générale des civilisations*, the other a German-inspired compilation, the *Historia Mundi*. Yet a paradox quickly emerged. Both in these publications and in those that followed in Germany, France, Britain and America, world history came into focus through a persistent national lens. In the *Histoire générale* we learn that 'l'histoire n'est pas choix, mais reconstitution de tous les aspectes de la vie'; and these turn out to be 'surtout . . . les formes economiques et sociales',[157] just as Braudel would have wished. For Jacques Pirenne, in his *Tides of History*, the problem was Barraclough's.

> Confronted by the abyss into which humanity has fallen, should we not take stock and examine our consciences? There is no other way to do so, in my opinion, than to follow, through the universal history of the first six thousand years of man, the long adventure of humanity.
>
> (Pirenne [1944–56]: 9–10)

The language, however, was not Barraclough's but, again, that of post-*Annales* inclusiveness, with a nod at Vico and Comte and even – he was searching for 'scientific and moral conclusions' – at Voltaire. The German studies similarly found that they could no more forget Sybel and Treitschke than Hitler; or at least they clung to a form of *Weltgeschichte* whose starting-point was novel – the sinking of the *Mutterkontinent* (see Randa 1954) – but whose vocabulary echoed traditional exponents of the art such as Hans Delbrück whose monumental series of lectures in Berlin had appeared in print as his five-volume *Weltgeschichte* during the 1920s.[158] In Britain the subject had become so stained by the speculations of Arnold Toynbee about the presence of cycles in world development that professional historians, as John Roberts complained when he turned to the subject of world history in 1976, had simply let it alone.[159] For Americans, meanwhile, the subject degenerated often into a bland 'World Civs' module

---

157 *Histoire générale des civilisations*, ed. Maurice Crouzet (7 vols, Paris, 1955–7), ix, xi. Cf. *Historia Mundi: ein Handbuch der Weltgeschichte*, ed. Fritz Valjavec (10 vols, Berne, 1952–61).
158 Delbrück 1924–8. He had been a pupil of Sybel. See Bentley 1997, ch. 11.
159 Roberts 1976: 9. For Toynbee, see Toynbee 1934–61 and McNeill 1989.

through which generations of students were required to plough until William McNeill grasped the subject and pulled it away towards an interesting and challenging way of thinking, not about the history of the world but rather about an enquiry called world history which had its own distinctive purpose and method. The recent establishment of a seminar in London entitled 'Global History in the Long Run' implies that this story is far from over.

If the war reconfigured the historians' sense of geography, it also transformed their awareness of technology. Partly this expanding horizon emerged from the progress made in communications generally: it became harder to pretend that Latin America or India or China needed no history when their images appeared regularly on television or documentary film. But overwhelmingly the harbinger of major change appeared through a revolution in computer technology resting on the need to counter Hitler's rocket programme and acquire a master-weapon in the atomic bomb. The genius of Alan Turing, the advanced calculations brought to the United States by Hitler's propulsion scientists, and the need to control and manipulate massive banks of data pressed forward the construction of computers whose utility for historians was as yet dimly perceived but which would make possible types of enquiry which no previous generation had been in a position to attempt. And from the mid-1950s onwards, these opportunities have given rise to styles of analysis which have altered the shape of historical argument in some fields. Three of these have proved especially remarkable: the 'new' economic history; the analysis of demography and family reconstitution; and the rise of a retrospective psephology which has given the conventional world of political history a distinctive turn.

We have seen that economic history had been part of the historiography of the West since at least the rise of the German school in the last third of the nineteenth century. It had shaken hands with Marxism, encouraged the theoretical models of Weber and had a shot in the arm from the economic catastrophes of 1929–33. When Bloch finally fought his way to a Parisian chair, it was a chair of economic history that he acquired.[160] The proliferation of professional periodicals such as the

---

160 For the circumstances surrounding Bloch's appointment at the Sorbonne, see Fink 1989: 185–7.

Economic History Review (1927) and others in Europe had already, by 1945, given the subject status and made it possible for the establishment of separate departments of economic history in the universities with a stress on the history of modern industrialization. In Britain this would give rise to prominent names that became quite as familiar as those of political historians : Clapham, needless to say, but also C. R. Fay, W. H. B. Court, Sidney Pollard. In France the thrust of *Annales* ran alongside economic investigation in the tradition of Simiand and Labrousse. Where a significant departure occurred in the 1950s was in the United States where some articles by Conrad and Meyer helped prompt a style of analysis that would attract the unlovely label 'cliometrics'. This approach had two central features: the collection of economic data covering long periods and in forms that a computer could manipulate; and the building of models against which to test hypotheses about economic variables within certain historical problems. The models attracted criticism and indeed notoriety for their being 'counter-factual'. They claimed to present a picture of what would have happened, if particular items in a historical complex had not been present or had been phased differently – a form of speculation that gave rise to indigestion among empiricists but which has also caused theorists some insomnia.[161] For its enthusiasts, the ability to control vast flows of quantitative information rendered conventional economic history out of date and immediately questioned all forms of history that could not provide precise quantification for their evidence. 'How many?', 'Have you counted?': these became the 1960s questions.

But of course the new mood went beyond that. Sir John Clapham (d.1946), the doyen of British economic historians, had always insisted on quantitative precision; computers merely made the task easier in one sense. Quite different from Clapham's teaching, indeed contrary to it, was a fashion in the United States for linking economic history to economic theory in a sub-Weberian way. There were to be ideal types, but the computer was to generate them, taking the historian's mind away from conventional reliance on isolated accounts (these were 'anecdotal') and supplementing historical portraiture ('impressionistic')

---

161 Some of the problems and opportunities are critically reviewed by Hawthorne 1991: 1–37.

with a quantitative method that ought to yield objective results through their very mass, rather in the way that Durkheim had thought that statistics contained a true history if only it could be divined. No sharp divide marks off 'old' from 'new' economic history; but one could certainly nominate as highly symptomatic of its central tenets an article by Conrad and Meyer in 1958. This aimed to show whether slave-ownership on Southern plantations was profitable in the *ante-bellum* period, but it performed this task by using statistical and computational techniques that had gained currency over the previous few years and on the basis of historical sources that seemed to many as random as they were slight. In retrospect, however, the article took on a pioneering quality because it seemed to adumbrate the more celebrated enquiry prosecuted by Fogel and Engerman in 1974, which appeared under the title *Time on the Cross*.

Fogel came at the subject of slavery from the direction of more conventional problems relating to the economic structure of America during the nineteenth century. His study of the railway system's impact on growth deployed the model-building and counter-factual propositions that were to become integral to his later work (Fogel 1964; compare, on the methodologies involved, Fogel 1966). But the book on slavery touched nerves that the earlier publications had not – partly because of the obvious technical problems facing anyone trying to reconstruct a balance sheet using data derived from so oral and informal a society, yet more, perhaps, because historians wedded to history as a *Geisteswissenschaft* found themselves reacting almost out of aesthetic revulsion in seeing an area of human tragedy and humiliation reduced to a spreadsheet evaluated by 'systematic statistical tests' (Fogel and Engerman 1974: I, 10) rather than the educated eye. It seemed a history untouched by human hand. This was undoubtedly unfair and Fogel was right to see such criticisms as missing the point of the enquiry. In a later debate with G. R. Elton, he rounded on critics of cliometrics with an argument that we can take as a definition:

> The common characteristic of cliometricians is that they apply the quantitative methods and behavioral models of the social sciences to the study of history.... Cliometricians want the study of history to be based on explicit models of human behavior. They believe that historians do not really have a choice of using or not using behavioral models since all attempts to explain historical behavior – to relate the elemental facts of

history to each other – . . . involve some sort of model. The real choice is whether these models will be implicit, vague, incomplete and internally inconsistent, as cliometricians contend is frequently the case in traditional historical research, or whether the models will be explicit, with all the relevant assumptions clearly stated, and formulated in such a manner as to be subject to rigorous empirical verification.

(Fogel and Elton 1983: 24–6)

This clarity of exposition did not prevent the savaging of *Time on the Cross*: indeed its very starkness helped stimulate a battery of assaults on and defences of the idea of cliometrics through the 1970s and 1980s.[162]

The debate between Fogel and the arch–empiricist Elton proved that they believed basically the same thing: they disagreed about the place of social science but they agreed that the point of historical work was to uncover some historical 'truth' by a process of discovery and reconstruction. Curiously, the French historical establishment, by now a virtual tyranny of *bien pensants* dominated by Braudel, went in the same direction. This was odd because much of the theoretical under-pinning of the *annaliste* enterprise turned on representing history as an act of imaginative construction rather than the reporting of a given state of affairs that historical work somehow uncovered. Yet in their enthusiasm for the computer (who can forget Le Roy Ladurie's remark that the historian of the future will be a programmer or he or she will be nothing?) the *dévôts* of Paris moved towards a development of cliometrics which their guru, Pierre Chaunu, decided to call 'serial history'. Building on the methodological recommendations of a sociologist, Jean Marczewski, in 1965, this approach seeks to go beyond the archive and extend the base from which historians can work by constructing series or runs of data calculated at regular intervals, say at yearly logging-points, over long periods – often a century or more. The point seems to be the resurrection of a hidden 'historical reality' which can only be grasped quantitatively and only tested statistically. Here is François Furet in definitional mood:

[T]he most general and at the same time the most elementary ambition of quantitative history is to set out historical reality in temporal series of homogeneous and comparable units, and in that way to measure the evolution of that reality at given intervals, usually annual. This fundamental

---

162 For an excellent introduction to the material available, see Fogel 1964: 24–6, n.17.

logical operation is definitional of what Pierre Chaunu has called serial history . . . [This] has the decisive advantage from a scientific point of view of replacing the ineffable 'events' of positivist history with the regular repetition of data selected and constructed because of their comparable nature. . . . The distribution of historical reality into series presents the historian with materials broken up into different levels, into different sub-systems, and he is then free to establish or not to establish connections between these levels.

(Furet 1984: 14)

Needless to say, the empowered historians have indeed 'established' connections and produced a formidable historiography relating to climate and demography as well as to economic history. The problem remains the one that arose in the United States – one about the funda-mental ambitions of historical work and the conceptual thought-world in which they are set.[163]

This objection did not operate in the domain of demography. For here the ability of a computer designed to make use of silicon-chip technology rather than punch-cards[164] to handle the vast runs of data available in, for example, modern census reports operated as an extension of human memory to allow a form of analysis that no human could perform. Beginning in France in the 1950s, the impetus reached Britain with the foundation in 1964 of the Cambridge Group for the History of Population and Social Structure.[165] Those connected with that group such as Peter Laslett, whose *The World We Have Lost* made a considerable stir when it appeared, and E. A. Wrigley, whose work has reorientated understanding of British demographic history since the early modern period, have made a major difference to the way in which problems not only of global demographic data but also of the microcosm of family reconstitution are approached.[166] Similarly social historians such as Michael Anderson have transformed the way in which nineteenth-century population history is tackled through their

---

163 For an American perspective on the French developments, see Tilly 1972.
164 Non-initiates are guided to Hull 1992. Cf. Lukoff 1979; Evans 1983 for a history of the computer.
165 For some details see Barraclough 1978: 77f.
166 Peter Laslett's central work in demography, apart from *The World We Have Lost*, is *A Fresh Map of Life; the Emergence of the Third Age* (1996). Cf. Bonfield et al. 1986. For E. A. Wrigley, see Wrigley 1987; 1988; Wrigley and Schofield 1989.

insistence on sophisticated quantification. Anderson's sample of the 1851 census in Britain comments on the astonishing detail that the computer makes available to researchers, because of the ability to code data in ways that make retrieval not only possible but simple in styles of search that would have taken previous generations years to attempt and which they would have ruled out of the enquiry on that ground.[167]

Some of the same thrust has become apparent in political analysis, too, though historians have not always found it possible to feel enthusiastic. Psephology – the study of elections and voting behaviour – certainly has benefited. British experience in particular suggests a clear future for such work in face of the use made by analysts such as Frank O'Gorman (1989) and the American scholar John A. Philipps (1982) of quantitative method as a way of investigating the pre-1832 British electorate. Presented with 'poll books', which are collections of printed information about how people voted in the years before the secret ballot was introduced in 1872, the historian can do little with the naked eye: the columns of material form too complex a block of information to allow one to see patterns in it. A simple software package into which the information may be keyed allows one to go beyond this confinement; the machine is able to search along axes established by the author, identify cases that fit the stated criteria and present the information in accordance with any variable named. Even the most Luddite of archival scholars finds it hard to resist the usefulness of such a device when once it is demonstrated. Of course the familiar GIGO – garbage in, garbage out – applies in political history quite as strongly as elsewhere. Roderick Floud, whose work in quantitative history has been of seminal importance in Britain over the past two decades (Floud 1979; cf. Floud and McCloskey 1994) rightly remarks that it may well be the case that one could correlate parliamentary division lists with phases of the moon. Achieving the correlation would not turn it into an intelligent operation (Floud 1979: ch. 7) – a thought some would like to see translated into French. For this reason one wonders sometimes about the point of focusing on sources such as division lists in the British Parliament as the source for quantitative analysis, though that has not prevented extensive work

---

167 See Anderson's guide to the records: Anderson 1987. See also Anderson 1980.

from being done on them (see e.g. Aydelotte 1971; 1972; 1977). As in other areas where quantification has become fashionable, much depends on a personal reading of the 'scientific' nature of history. And as in other areas of personal experience, the national often determines the personal: it is no accident that American scholars still turn more readily to the silicon chip than do scholars working in more conventional cultures.

14

THE HISTORY OF THE PRESENT

The 1960s acquired an historiographical mood. It was nothing so tight as an agenda, far less a list of specified topics or approaches. But it wanted answers, crystalline conclusions, whether they came as numbers or prosaic certainties. Like most moments that imagine themselves to have found keys to long-closed doors, it welcomed science and baptized various styles of positivism: *annaliste*, *marxisant*, anthropological, archaeological, sociological, ideologically correct, emotionally committed. It was a self-conscious decade in a way and to a degree that the despised 1950s had never aspired to be; and it nurtured an earnest view of its own importance that the 1970s and 1980s never sought. Amid the trials of Cuba and Vietnam, the Prague Spring and the Paris Spring, it depicted itself as the beginning of something significant in social and historical enquiry. It was right about its significance, wrong about its beginning. For the 1960s seem from the 1990s not a departure but an arrival. The decade became the terminus of modernism.

Understanding 'modernism' matters if only to help sort out what we ought to understand by 'postmodernism', which has become the slogan for so much since. Modernist views may perhaps best be seen as a cluster of positions relating to philosophy, literary analysis, aesthetics and all the social sciences between, very roughly, 1910 and 1970. The views themselves ranged widely in content and application, but they seem united by a particular tone that implied the availability of truth, the undesirability of metaphysics and all forms of blurredness, the necessity for rationalism of an Enlightenment kind. From the two theories of relativity to the double helix of DNA, from the sociology of Talcott Parsons to the anthropology of Claude Lévi-Strauss, the texts of modernism breathed the excitement of discovery, the identification of hidden structures, the digging-up of clues and Sutton Hoos.[168] Historians did not believe themselves to be modernists because they rarely believe themselves to be anything worth a label. But their enquiries, beyond the subversion of a few sceptics like the brilliant but baffling Michael Oakeshott, had the modernist feel for realizable truth and a consistent implication that the past was out there as a visitable place. 'The past is a foreign country; they do things differently there.'[169] This modernist remark says exactly what modernists believed and what postmodernists do not.

The certainties and the discoveries extended to politics. Chief among the 1960s certainties came a from-the-heart leftism which denounced imperialist wars, espoused a youth culture in dress and music, and dallied with soft drugs. In West Germany sizeable proportions of the undergraduate population removed themselves from any form of democratic politics and threatened radically to destabilize the most hierarchical academic system in Europe. This mood intersected in Britain with what in retrospect seems the high point of historical Marxism. Most of the original members of the Communist Party Historians' Group, formed just after the war, had left the party after the crushing of Hungary's liberation movement in 1956. But the message of Christopher Hill, Eric Hobsbawm and above all E. P. Thompson, whose *The Making of the English Working Class* (1963) became the cynosure of its generation, mixed easily with the 1950s populism of Richard Hoggart and Raymond Williams,[170] maintaining through the incendiary pages of the *New Left Review*, meanwhile, a

168 Sutton Hoo in Suffolk, England, is a well-remarked archaeological site containing a longboat of *circa* the seventh century, discovered in 1939.

169 The often-recalled opening words of L. P. Hartley's novel *The Go-Between*. Cf. Lowenthal 1985.

170 Richard Hoggart (b.1918) became best known for *The Uses of Literacy* (1957) and Williams (1921–88) for *Culture and Society* (1958).

dialogue with Perry Anderson in the United States and Louis Althusser in France (see Bentley 1997, ch. 36). It was a time to *épater les bourgeois*. Sometimes those doing the shocking found themselves shocked in turn by a form of 'revisionism' that reversed the prevailing colours; and it is noticeable how some very fundamental rethinking of historical problems took place in reaction to the changed mood, whether it was A. J. P. Taylor's (1961) denial of Hitler's 'blue-print' for a war in 1939, or the denial by Ronald Robinson (1961) and John Gallagher of the Marxist thesis of imperialism in Africa (Robinson *et al.* 1961), or the denial by Maurice Cowling (1967) of the Marxist thesis about the importance of the English working class in 1867. It even provoked a clever book denying certainty itself (Letwin 1965).

At some point in the 1970s, whatever held together a prevalent intellectual environment of this sort changed and changed utterly. Chronologically the shift ran alongside a major political one in the West away from socialist planning and towards free-market economics associated with political leadership such as that of Ronald Reagan and Margaret Thatcher. Perhaps the relation between these two levels of discussion went beyond fellow-travelling; certainly some observers found in the new mood an outgrowth of a particular stage of late capitalism (Jameson 1991; 1981). Yet whatever its initial conditions may have been, a developing sense of a 'turn' – the 'postmodern turn' – began to make itself felt in the social and literary theory of the period, strengthening and redefining through the 1980s and beyond. At first it may have seemed to practical historians that people had turned against 'science' (again). This is what Michael Postan seems to have picked up in 1971:

> Except for Marxists, most historians writing about the philosophy of history, most philosophers concerned with the methodology of historical and social study, and even some influential social anthropologists, have in recent years ranged themselves against the supposed fallacies of 'scientism'. They accept, however unconsciously, the idealistic dichotomy of 'physical' and 'humanistic' studies of that of pure and practical reason, and consequently decry all attempts to use the methods of natural science in the study of history or of human affairs in general.

> (Postan 1971: ix)

But of course it went further than that. New words appeared: 'post-structuralism'; 'deconstruction'; 'alterity'; 'textuality'; many others.

Historians chose normally not to use them; indeed few of them knew what any of them meant. Yet their periodicals, their weekly reviews and magazines, and, in increasing numbers, their monographic literature began to reflect a changing climate. It is witness to the pervasiveness of that environment that surveys of historiography, when they discuss changes in the tendencies of this recent period, often say little explicitly about postmodernism while implying volumes between their lines about its impact. The reticence is completely understandable. Postmodernism has made a major difference to historical projects now underway but does not yet itself have a historiography: we shall see much more clearly its historical ramifications in thirty or forty years' time. It has, all the same, a presence and a vocabulary that readers need to encounter and we ought not to conclude this survey of historiographical developments without considering them.

'Postmodern' is an adjective most helpfully attached to a particular phase or period of thought, as Jane Caplan suggests, rather than to a specific collection of tools or approaches.[171] Like 'enlightened' or 'romantic', it signals a persuasion that has obtained a partial grip on the speculations of a particular epoch. And like those designators, it provides only a broad clue to what any person falling within its ambit may believe. Some of the more obvious characteristics common among 'postmodern' writers include: a rejection, philosophically, of the self as a 'knowing subject' in the form presented in European thought after Kant and before Heidegger; an allied rejection of the possibility of finding a singular 'true' picture of the external world, present or past; a concern to 'decentre' and destabilize conventional academic subjects of enquiry; a wish to see canons of orthodoxy in reading and writing give way to plural readings and interpretations; a fascination with text itself and its relation to the reality it purports to represent; a drive to amplify previously unheard voices from unprivileged groups and peoples; a preoccupation with gender as the most immediate generator of underprivileged or unempowered status; a dwelling on power and lack of it as a conditioner of intellectual as much as political

---

171 I follow in this section the untangling of 'postmodern' from 'poststructural' in Professor Caplan's thoughtful and stimulating paper, Caplan 1989.

configurations within a culture. Each of these has begun to nibble at, sometimes bite on, the assumptions of working historians whose conscious activity may betray no shadow of interest in theoretical matters. To review each of them here would take the discussion away from the focus of this volume; but four clusters of questions have none the less impinged forcefully enough to warrant a word here, those surrounding poststructuralism and language, textuality and narrative, a feminist reading of the history of women, and the project of a 'new' cultural history.

Poststructuralism differs from postmodernism because it addresses itself to a specific mode of criticism arising out of linguistics and then tries to reverse and supersede it. It does not connote an atmosphere promoted by a particular period – its central ideas became available before the onset of a distinctive 'postmodern' environment – but rather a collection of insights provoked by a reaction against the idea that language consists of 'closed' structures. This latter view is normally associated with Saussure, though the writers we think of as structuralists ran far beyond Saussure's contentions. The insistence in Saussure that language operates as a constantly modifying but always complete system which generates meaning through complicated internal codes and symbols (instead of a one-to-one correspondence between words and things, signifier and signified) was expanded outside the sphere of linguistic and literary analysis to imply, in Caplan's words, that 'all cultural systems represent coded systems of meaning rather than direct transactions with reality' (1989: 265). But one could go further than that, and in doing so social theorists often exposed their modernist roots by claiming that these puzzles of meaning and codification could be solved. One could extract an answer; it was a question of cracking the code. It is not possible to read a structural anthropologist like Claude Lévi-Strauss, for example, without picking up that fundamental optimism and many of the historical works of the 1960s reflect some of the same tone. This was the position against which poststructuralists reacted. Among historians perhaps the most influential thinker involved in this reaction was the Parisian guru, Michel Foucault. It is not that Foucault was a historian himself or, if he were, he was a very bad one. Rather, his assertion of a relationship between power and knowledge reversed the familiar *mot* – power is knowledge rather than vice versa because power determines the conditions in which particular

141

knowledge-forms ('epistemes', as he called them) come into being and find sustenance. And by doing so it brought into question the familiar forms of knowledge brought to bear on the past by historians, forms which he implied reflected the power-distributions of their own societies to the detriment of plural readings of the past.[172] No one observer can ever encompass the 'truth' of a situation, this line of criticism alleged, which will appear differently to people with distinctive cultures imposing different points of view. Historiography has to make space, therefore, for the 'truths' of women, black people, Asian people, the inarticulate and dispossessed. In Caplan's formulation,

> [t]he poststructuralism advanced by the later [Roland] Barthes, [Jacques] Derrida, Foucault and others rejects the stability and closure of the structuralist system . . . and the proposition that the truth of a system is intelligible to an observer or reader who occupies the appropriate vantage point.

> (Caplan 1989: 266)

In so far as an historical truth is available at all, it becomes one whose validity can only apply in relation to the particular and limited vantage point from which it derives. The past disappears as an object and turns into a construct which must allow the validity of alternative constructions which can be tested only by criteria internal to the cultural and intellectual frameworks that generate them.

These alternative constructions do not take the form of structures fixed in time, as many pre-1970 texts might have displayed, but rather become narratives over time. In some ways, indeed, poststructural history can resemble in its textuality the historiography of the 1860s more closely than that of the 1960s. Yet there remains a crucial difference. Victorian narrative arranged itself as a fundamental story-line that gave an account of some great and overarching theme: the rise of the nation; the coming of greatness; the history of liberty. Postmodern narratives begin with the proposition that all such grand architecture is suspect at best. At worst, it confines historical accounts to an established canon of interpretation in order to prove by implication the presence of some persistent undertow. When Jean Lyotard wrote *The Postmodern Condition* (1984), possibly the first book self-consciously

---

172 For Foucault on power, see in particular Foucault 1966 and 1980. Cf. Megill 1985; Grumley 1989; Barker 1993.

to announce the beginning of a new era, he provided the shortest known definition of postmodernist assumption as a 'disbelief in meta-narratives'; and certainly the dismissal of historiography devoted to proving the reality of a single *Leitmotif* has become a theme of much poststructural criticism. There should be stories, lots of them. But they are to reflect a plurality of 'truths', not a single Authorized Version. Historical narrative is to be distinguished from fiction, moreover, by nothing so trivial as truth. Of course, historical narrative takes its form and content from certain controls implicit in the sort of material historians use; but it is not, in its postmodern raiment, to be seen as having a one-to-one correspondence with historical truth. It will function simply as one form of 'discourse' (Foucault's over-used and often misunderstood term) that one can place against other forms but never against the thing that all historical discourses consider: the past itself.[173] Peter Munz has given the issue a pungent formulation:

> We cannot glimpse at history. We can only compare one book with another book.... Historians alone among all scientists still believe that the only reason why truth eludes them is that they show too much bias, or that their sources do, or that there are missing 'facts'. But this is all wrong. The real reason why it must forever elude us is that it is not there. There is nothing the case over and above what people have thought (ie., the sources) and think (ie., the narratives), so that we can have no statement of which we can say that it is true if and only if what it asserts is the case.
>
> (Munz 1977)

For this reason, among others, the power of literary theory as a critique of common historical practice has become very noticeable since the 1970s.[174] Historians have watched or actively aided the unravelling of their discipline in order to cope better with new currents of thought and to bring their more recent subject matter into a better fit with modern thought.

One subject has exemplified this movement particularly clearly. The rise of 'gender' as an historiographical category has been as remarkable as it is recent, beginning with a politicized history of

---

173 Cf. Palmer 1989. Peter Munz deals with some of the issues in more detail in Bentley 1997, ch. 34.
174 Literary theory has affected historical thought in too many indirect ways to note here, but see Barthes 1977; Canary and Kozick 1978; Gossman 1990. See also n. 176 below.

women on the back of the female emancipation movement of the 1960s but turning into a genre that seeks to address the problem of female and male roles in past societies and thereby to unlock doors into a number of historical areas that conventional political and social history had left closed. To see the transition in this light offends those who deem 'this field . . . a dynamic study in the politics of knowledge production' (Scott 1992: 44) but there seems no obligation to think about the story in that way. It undoubtedly is the case that accounts of male–female relations in past societies now flourish without the patina of overt political recommendation that the early literature tended to deploy. All history has, ultimately, a political propulsion in that all stories begin from a standpoint. The tone of postmodernist speculation about gender seems no more political, on the other hand, than most other sectors of historical writing and it has recently adopted a mood of sub-scientific enquiry that would not so easily consort with an overt political stance.[175] The literature none the less concerns itself heavily with issues of identity which in turn raise painful questions about who should write history in this sphere. People sometimes say that only women, perhaps only some kind of women, are qualified to write women's history. The thought echoes in the proposition that only black people can write the history of black people; and so on in an infinite progress or regress. Each of these narratives, moreover, will take its place as another slab of discourse within which, seen from one modernist or structuralist direction, criticism will be internalized. It is hardly surprising that for one wing of the argument this kind of development marks a significant and necessary liberation from the tyranny of unsympathetic historical method. For another, it heralds the collapse of historical method of any kind, the dissolution of an intellectual discipline (in both senses) and a 'descent into discourse', as Bryan Palmer complains in his book of that title (1989). In Bentley 1997, chapter 37, Olwen Hufton offers a personal reflection of some of this story while in chapter 9 Janet Nelson shows how these perspectives come into play when historians look at a particular problem.

---

175 Fletcher 1995; Hufton 1995. Of course to some extent the divide may reflect an Anglo–American contrast. For bibliographical guidance on recent developments in this area of study, see Dauphin *et al.* 1986; Vickery 1993. I am grateful to Julia Smith for these latter references.

A similar concern with discourse, readings and texts dominates a strand of historiography to which the label of 'new cultural history' has been attached by the American scholar, Lynn Hunt (1989). Unlike the case of the new economic history, this mode is not a self-conscious one and it rather pulls together a series of disparate initiatives through the 1980s: work on reading, literacy and the history of the book (especially in the hands of the subject's first master, Roger Chartier (1987; 1993; 1994); analysis of narrative texts as a form, particularly the innovative thinking of Hayden White, Paul Ricœur and Dominick LaCapra;[176] anthropological views of micro-historical events, such as Robert Darnton's famous *The Great Cat Massacre* or Natalie Zemon Davis's well-known book *The Return of Martin Guerre*;[177] and the beginning of a theme dealing with social 'memory'.[178] Even these few instances suggest how different this approach to the study of a 'culture' is from the classical origins of *Kulturgeschichte* in Burckhardt and Huizinga. New cultural historians reflect often a cultural optimism and a picture of the proper concerns of social history that is avowedly 'inclusive' both socially and intellectually. They stand far away from the celebration of elites and the vision of a hierarchical society as the last bastion of civilization. Nor do they appear blind to some economic determinants, as both Burckhardt and Huizinga tended to be: witness the success of Martin Wiener's *English Culture and the Decline of the Industrial Spirit* (1981). Their methods and topics, equally, suggest innovation rather than the working-out of a former tradition; and these have an inter-continental as much as an inter-disciplinary feel. Just as one wing of

---

176 For Hayden White see in particular White 1973; 1987. Paul Ricœur's reputation was made in hermeneutics: for a representative selection, see Valdes 1991. There is a rather unsatisfactory published lecture on *The Reality of the Historical Past* (1984); but the main source for historians should be *Temps et recit*, which has been translated as *Time and Narrative* (1984-8). The thrust of LaCapra has been literary as much as historical, but there are helpful pieces in LaCapra 1983; 1985.

177 Robert Darnton's techniques of *microstoria* can be seen in *The Great Cat Massacre* (1984). Cf. his study of *The Corpus of Clandestine Literature in France 1769–89* (1995) and its sister volume, *The Forbidden Bestsellers of Pre-Revolutionary France* (1995). The fame of Natalie Zemon Davis was made by *The Return of Martin Guerre* (1983), but see also *Society and Culture in Early-Modern France: Eight Essays* (1975) and *Women on the Margins: Three Seventeenth-Century Lives* (1995).

178 Social 'memory': Fentress and Wickham 1992; Roth 1995.

new sensibility announced itself in a volume such as Quentin Skinner's influential *The Return of Grand Theory* in 1985, another threw off theory in order to pursue what became known in Italy as *microstoria*, which sometimes took the form of local or regional social history but which came to take on the character of a non-spatial concentration on a particular event or source in order to elucidate wider contexts. Carlo Ginzburg's *The Cheese and the Worms* of 1980 famously reconstructed the thought-world of a sixteenth-century miller and opened a decade of Italian concern with specific contexts reflected in the work, for example, of Giovanni Levi.[179] This work echoes the best-selling account of *Montaillou* by the *annaliste*, Emmanuel Le Roy Ladurie (1978) (cf. Le Roy Ladurie 1984), which likewise showed what might be wrung from a collection of tightly organized material relating to a single series of events in a locality. The American version of cultural history took much of its tone originally from France, also; and as one thinks across territory in considering the historiography of the 1980s a fault-line seemingly wanders across it, dividing the historical approaches of France, Italy and America but uniting parts of those environments in a common tendency.

French tendencies affected Britain less markedly and Germany hardly at all. Perhaps the British case makes sense when one considers not only its traditional empiricism and hostility to over-conceptualized argument, but also the lack of *Kulturgeschichte* as a national trait, beyond the history of art pioneered in the Warburg Institute. The German resistance to this new mood is harder to explain. In a tradition of scholarship that included Lamprecht, and his long-standing friendship with Pirenne, one might expect to find a readier response. Yet in fact the Rhine, as one observer pointed out a decade ago, became an intellectual frontier just as it had functioned as a territorial one since 1870. The lack of mutual interest between French and German historiography after 1945 seems little less than astonishing. It is not that Germany persisted in a state-dominated, political historiography: one could argue that West Germany gave rise to a school of important

---

179 Ginzburg 1980; 1983; 1991; Levi 1988. Cf. Ginzburg's essays collected in English as *Myths, Emblems, Clues* (1990) and Levi's reflections 'On Microhistory' in Burke 1992: 93–113. I am grateful to Professor Chris Wickham for his guidance here. For the wider context of Italian historiography, see Bentley 1997, ch. 22.

social history based in Bielefeld, inspired by Werner Conze and Hans-Ulrich Wehler and drawing on a depth of work in social history that ran back into Weimar and the Nazi period.[180] But the questions asked never moved in the direction of *annalisme*; and the various emphases of *le monde Braudelien* found little sympathy from Berlin and Heidelberg. The French, conversely, did not write about Germany to nearly the extent that British and American historians have done – a point stressed by Hartmut Kaelble in a revealing analysis of the difference between the two cultures. In seeking the distinctiveness of the German experience he notes a number of points of contrast, three of which seem fundamental: the German concern with history as a form of political education – unavoidable granted German memories since 1933 – contrasting with the French mood of transcending traditional categories in a way that leaves its historians '*politikfern*', distant from political concerns; a German interest in change and process, contrasting with a growing French stress on unchanging or slowly changing structures, on *durée* rather than *l'histoire événementielle*; and finally a German preoccupation with theory as a leading category rather than what often seems a romantic or rhetorical decoration for the hands-on practices of the *Annales*. If the Germans have failed to find a Braudel or a Duby, the French have not sought to produce a Reinhart Kosellek or Jörn Rüsen.[181] For all these reasons the structuralist ideas associated with a 'modernist' disposition better suited the temperament and background of German historians, especially granted the powerful Marxist tradition of analysis which, of course, was mandatory in East Germany until the coming of unification. Even when the Berlin Wall came down in 1989, the ensuing euphoria produced not a ripple of cultural history in the *Historische Zeitschrift*.

Historiography is not a form of prediction and only a fool would assert where these various trends will go. The best platform for speculation perhaps lies in studies of concrete instances and some of the

---

180 Conze 1963; 1964; 1967; his later work on social history has mostly been editorial, though voluminous. Wehler's output has been enormous and centres currently on his continuing *Deutsche Gesellschaftsgeschichte*. But see also the *Festschrift* for his sixtieth birthday: Hettling *et al.* 1991.

181 Koselleck *et al.* 1982; Koselleck 1985; Rüsen 1983–6. An exception on the French side is the late Michel de Certeau: see esp. Certeau 1988.

more thoughtful critics have taken the opportunity to think ahead and wonder about the direction of their specialism over the next few years. Meanwhile so much in the current context appears undigested. Postmodernism as an intellectual form is already provoking a backlash. The consequences for the writing of history of the crash of communism in 1989 have not yet begun to work themselves out, though we can certainly remain sceptical in face of arguments about the End of Ideology, the End of History and the Beginning of Post-History (see Bell 1960; Fukuyama 1992; Niethammer, 1992). The discipline has survived several political revolutions and two world wars: it ought to be able to cope with Mr Gorbachev. National identities still inform all versions of historiography, sometimes in indirect ways. Indeed we seem still to be using history as the early nineteenth century did, as a vehicle for locating groups and peoples and giving them a past that suits their present or encourages their sense of a future. All of these things may alter. But one development in the history of the present looks likely to be both permanent and valuable. Historians have never been so *aware* of what they are attempting as they have become over the past two decades. Always a reflective form of writing, history has become (as they say) 'reflexive': it is self-conscious to a degree and to a level of sophistication that no previous generation can match with the partial exception of that of Carlyle and Humboldt. Possibly historians will become morbid and self-destructive as a result. Not a few have already become self-important. Yet the move towards a deliberately constructed history gives critics of all persuasions the opportunity and the duty to keep their swords sharp against a moment when contingencies may threaten to destroy the discipline or subvert an interest in the past at all. We shall do well to remember that historiography forms the stone that whets the blade.

POSTSCRIPT

This essay has sought to present an interpretative outline of some major themes in modern historiography. Selection and brevity have taken their toll, inevitably, and historians will find little difficulty in identifying several areas of considerable contemporary concern that were excluded. Two linked motives lay behind these exclusions. First, the study was written in its original form to supply context for other, more detailed accounts; it followed that topics could be glossed lightly or left out where they would become the subject of other contributions. Second, the conception of the work turned on a history of historical writing rather than a summary of contemporary movements or prophecy about the historical future. It is hoped that readers who wish to expand their understanding of some of the issues merely glanced at in this account will return to the larger *Companion to Historiography* and perhaps make use of the suggestions for further reading suggested both there and at the end of this postscript. But the issuing of this statement in a free-standing format gives an opportunity to point to certain aspects of the contemporary situation which, although they have not yet given rise to a mature historiography, have already exerted considerable force on the direction of recent historical thinking and which promise to dominate the projects of historians in at least the immediate future. Evaluating those trends is itself a speculative act: other historians would see different shapes on the horizon. Uncertainty comes with the exercise, on the other hand, and seems no good reason for avoiding it altogether.

We have seen the sense of finality that accompanied the collapse of Communist Europe after 1989 and its accompanying *End of History* confidence. It has not lasted. Looking around the globe in 1998, the apparent crumbling of South-East Asia's capitalist miracle, its consequences for the economies of Japan and Australia and repercussions, in a globalized financial structure, as far away as New York and London give little credence to the brave new world of liberal capitalism announced by Fukuyama in 1992.[1] Continuing eruptions of nationalist *Angst* in the Balkan peninsula, with impending tragedy in the region of Kosovo, reflect in an extreme form a more general malaise about ethnicity and identity, prompting the thought that the peoples of the West have entered as much a period of doubt and questioning as one characterized by serenity. The political mood of the anglophone world, emphasized by the re-election of Clinton and the coming to power of Blair in Britain, increasingly appears a rhetorical construction: the smiles betray false teeth that so far have shown little ability to bite on the structural problems of both societies. Intellectually, too, one can detect a backlash against the cuddly correctnesses of postmodernism and an impatience with a vocabulary that often has not led anywhere. Does any critical historian exist who has not wanted to scream at the thousandth mention of 'discourse' when listening to conference papers? The rejection has now reached print, too – particularly among writers wishing to defend an older empiricism and rail against a sense of intellectual inertia.[2] On the philosophical level a parallel outlook has begun to emerge. Defences of 'realism' in theories of historical knowledge have sharply rejected the postmodern assumption that knowledge is ultimately unobtainable and tried to conserve the possibility of an historical enquiry that does more than talk about the 'coherence' of an interpretation but insists rather on moving beyond such paleness to make a claim instead about 'truth'.[3] It is too early to say whether this

---

1 Francis Fukuyama, *The End of History and the Last Man* (1992).

2 See in particular John Vincent, *An Intelligent Person's Guide to History* (1995) and Richard J. Evans, *In Defence of History* (1997).

3 Fundamental here from a philosophical point of view is Susan Haack, *Evidence and*

turn of mind heralds a revival of positivism of a 1960s kind, but instinct says that it will not.

In so far as postmodern concerns and questions have informed the creation of a new historiography, they have done so most powerfully, perhaps, within two clusters – one relating to subject matter, the other to method. Issues surrounding the concepts of identity and social memory comprise the first cluster. The reception and deployment of oral history and theories of narrative make up the second. In practice, the language associated with identity and memory reappears in discussion of oral history and narrative. Those interested in any aspect tend to share an interest in all. Indeed, one worry about this entire pattern is that it readily becomes a closed configuration with a circular style of argument. Identity is reinforced by an alleged social memory which most tellingly reveals itself in oral history and requires for its most sensitive exposition the telling of a distinctive story.

Yet each element resolves itself into a compound on closer examination. 'Identity' rests on a number of bases relating to nation, ethnic group and gender, plus a wide range of cultural confirmations and stimuli. Historians have worked with all of these notions over the last decade. The historiography of contemporary nationalism shows a movement away from the traditional array of state-led developments that might have informed, for example, a study of Bismarckian nationalism.[4] Following the impetus of an influential social scientist such as Anthony D. Smith, the place of ethnicity has come strongly to the fore, with present-day 'nationalism' often finding itself distinguished from the nineteenth-century variant, not always persuasively.[5] Historians have breathed a certain amount of anthropological ozone – it would have been hard to escape it in the later 1980s and through the next decade – and the bookshops now groan under the weight of *Readers* that both capture the mood and preach inter-disciplinarity.[6] Benedict

---

Inquiry: Towards Reconstruction in Epistemology (Cambridge, Mass., 1993). For historical thinkers proceeding along a similar path, see Martin Bunzl, *Real History: Reflections on Historical Practice* (1997) and C. Beehan McCullagh, *The Truth of History* (1998).

4 An exception is John Breuilly, *Nationalism and the State* (Manchester, 1993).

5 For Eric Hobsbawm, see note 9. For Smith, cf. his *National Identity* (1991).

6 At random one might alight on John Shotter and Kenneth J. Gergen (eds), *Texts of*

Anderson gave a considerable push to the nationalism-as-ideology persuasion in his *Imagined Communities* (1991) which replaced material forces as explanatory agents, with the exception of printing which he took to be a crucial precondition of nationalism, by the notion of mental projection.[7] Coupled with the grievous experience of Serbia and Croatia, these tendencies represented 1980s xenophobias as the expression of a crisis in historical identity – a disturbing form of *anomie* about which historians could say a great deal. They then, of course, turned around, faced backwards into their own periods of the past and applied what was happening around them as a way of re-negotiating, say, nineteenth-century nationalism or the origins of the First World War.[8] By the time Adrian Hastings came to deliver his Wiles Lectures in The Queen's University, Belfast, in 1996, the tone had shifted markedly from when Hobsbawm delivered them on the same theme a decade earlier.[9] One has only to consider the nouns in Hastings' published version – *The Construction of Nationhood: Ethnicity, Religion and Nationalism* – to sense the terms within which national identity now found its location.[10]

But identity concerns individuals as well as collectivities and here, too, a discernible mood of 'social-construction' has made itself apparent. Ever since Durkheim, an argument about the manufacture of the individual by the society of which (s)he forms a part can be detected, as we saw in earlier sections of this essay, under the surface of analysis in sociology and anthropology. The crude determinism of this undertow found little favour among devotees of *Posthistoire*. Their interest in cultural formations and responses to gender and race none

---

Identity (1989); Montserrat Guibernau and John Rex (eds), *The Ethnicity Reader: Nationalism, Multiculturalism and Migration* (Cambridge, 1997).

7 Benedict Anderson, *Imagined Communities: Reflections on the Origin and Spread of Nationalism* (1991).

8 Morse Peckham, *Beyond the Tragic Vision: A Quest for Identity in the Nineteenth Century* (Cambridge, 1981); Seamus Dunn and T. G. Fraser, *Europe and Ethnicity: The First World War and Contemporary Ethnic Conflict* (1996).

9 Eric Hobsbawm, *Nation and Nationalism since 1780: Programme, Myth, Reality* (Cambridge, 1990). The lectures were delivered in 1985.

10 Hastings, *op. cit.* (Cambridge, 1997). Note the nouns and date, too, in T. K. Oommen, *Citizenship, Nationality and Ethnicity: Reconciling Competing Identities* (Cambridge, 1997).

the less pressed forward investigation of how social immersion played a part in configuring personal outlooks and ideologies. At its most arresting this viewpoint might reconsider the definition of the self as an idea – prompting an historical consideration of how selfhood changes over time and portraying it less as a given or tangible thing than as a fluid 'representation', a postmodern term with multiple resonances. The revised narrative would eschew 'progress' as its central dynamic. 'The notion of an ascent', Roy Porter argued in 1997, 'from some primordial collective psychological soup to a sharply defined individual identity now seems a question-begging and self-serving leftover of Victorian fanfares of progress.'[11] A similar project entered the historiography of gender. Originally overwhelmed by the history of women (a related but quite different subject) and given the political spin that Joan Wallach Scott and her *consoeurs* imparted on it during the liberationist phase of the 1960s and early 1970s, the idea gained much ground of a gender-based history resting on more neutral questions about how men and women relate to one another across time and circumstance, and in doing so how they construct their particular identities.

An interest in the body itself and the degree to which conceptions of its functions alter the sense of self made itself felt in the 1990s. Basic to this analytical structure was Peter Brown's *The Body and Society*, which allowed the tensions posed by the ideal of chastity to lead the argument of a complex book about the nature of early Christian practice.[12] The argument owed its usual debt to Brown's imaginative brilliance and little to theoretical propositions. These appeared two years later in a far more controversial piece of Durkheimian construction in the United States. Thomas Laqueur had already collaborated on *The Making of the Modern Body*[13] whose constuctionist mood foreshadowed Laqueur's theorizing of the history of the body and the implications of various conceptions of anatomy for gender relations in

---

11 Roy Porter (ed.), *Rewriting the Self: Histories from the Renaissance to the Present* (1997), p. 9.
12 Peter Brown, *The Body and Society: Men, Women and Sexual Renunciation in Early Christianity* (New York, 1988).
13 Catherine Gallagher and Thomas Laqueur, *The Making of the Modern Body: Sexuality and Society in the Nineteenth Century* (Berkeley, 1987).

the West from classical times to the present.[14] This caused a stir among both feminists and their enemies and precipitated serious criticism of a line of argument that appeared to limit and abbreviate female consciousness to the acknowledgement of a physical imperative. Again, the insights, if such they were, served as encouragement to open new periods and contexts and within a few years Brown's message for antiquity had been amplified as the early modernists explored their bodies.[15] The history of women reflected some of these concerns, moving on from Denise Riley's *Am I That Name?*[16] into the highly sophisticated histories of female consciousness and role in Europe among which Olwen Hufton's history may be seen as a flagship, and Anthony Fletcher's redeployment of Laqueur's perspectives in the early modern history of England.[17] Language associated with identity has come to dominate the literature, however, and current titles reflect an increasing interaction with a more general discussion – *Women, Identity and Private Life*, for example, or *Gender, Ethnicities and Political Ideologies*.[18] It is as though the history of identity, conceived as a starting-point, has modulated through the 1990s into an attempt at historical definition of what once had been assumed. Identity now figures as the end of a complicated process of construction – subtle, malleable and evolving.

Part of the complication comes with memory. This difficulty can be seen at once within an individual's memory, even when we assume that such a recollected past is entirely that of the remembering subject's, with no social or cultural interference. Everybody has had experience of

---

14 Thomas Laqueur, *Making Sex: Body and Gender from the Greeks to Freud* (Cambridge, Mass., 1990).

15 E.g. Dominic Montserrat, *Changing Bodies, Changing Meanings: Studies on the Human Body in Antiquity* (1998); Marjo Kaartinen and Ann Korhonen, *Bodies in Evidence: Perspectives on the History of the Body in Early Modern Europe* (Turku, 1997).

16 Denise Riley, *Am I that Name? Feminism and the Category of 'Women' in History* (Basingstoke, 1988).

17 Olwen Hufton, *The Prospect before Her: A History of Women in Western Europe*, vol 1, 1500–1800 (1995); Anthony Fletcher, *Gender, Sex and Subordination in England 1500–1800* (New Haven, Conn., 1995).

18 Judy Giles, *Women, Identity and Private Life in Britain 1900–1950* (Basingstoke, 1995); Nickie Charles and Helen Hintjens, *Gender, Ethnicities and Political Ideologies* (1998).

hearing 'memories' which the documentary record can show to have been mistaken: dates telescoped or inverted, imagined witnessing of events which the subject could never have witnessed, moods conjured up – the perpetual sunshine of childhood, for example – which documentary historians can easily subvert. These problems undermine the claim of memory to provide a direct link with the past or a pulling of it forward into the present. Yet the difficulties go deeper. It is possible to argue that individual memory is itself a social construct, the product of our class, race, television, the newspaper we read and so on. This idea goes back essentially to Maurice Halbwachs, the colleague of Bloch and Febvre at Strasburg, in the 1920s. Strengthened in the following decade by a British psychologist, Sir Frederic Bartlett, this idea acquired a modern theoretical formulation in a polemical work by James Fentress and Chris Wickham in 1992.[19] The concept of 'social memory' has in fact many dubious aspects, not least through its use of the term 'memory' for operations which involve no recollection; and a sloppy way of thinking about this issue has now rather confused 'history', especially national history, with a form of collective memory, as though what historians do has a significant relationship with what recollection does. It actually makes more sense to invert that view: history is precisely non-memory, a systematic discipline which seeks to rely on mechanisms and controls quite different from those which memory triggers and often intended to give memory the lie. Nor is it at all clear that individual memory functions as the sub-set of a social construction. Plainly everyone's memory is affected by their social contacts. Equally plainly the act of *co*-memoration calls on social mechanisms for its being practised at all. But the recent *genre* which blurs together history, commemoration and individual remembering needs to be treated with a certain caution.[20] None the less memory has become a spectacular

---

19 Frederic Bartlett, *Remembering: A Study in Experimental and Social Psychology* (Cambridge, 1932); James Fentress and Chris Wickham, *Social Memory* (Oxford, 1992). 20 Among a long list of recent studies in this area, see Jacques Le Goff, *History and Memory* (New York, 1992); Patrick H. Hutton, *History as an Art of Memory* (Hanover, Vt, 1993); Michael S. Roth, *The Ironist's Cage: Memory, Trauma and the Construction of History* (New York, 1995); Patrick J. Geary, *Phantasms of Remembrance: Memory and Oblivion at the End of the First Millennium* (Princeton, NJ, 1994); Chris Healey, *From the Ruins of Colonialism: History as Social Memory* (Cambridge, 1997).

historical industry with journals such as *History and Memory*, a deeply-felt historiography relating to memories of the Holocaust and many conferences and congresses, such as the Royal Historical Society's conference on memory, oral history and written record in the spring of 1998.

The link between memory and orality, on the one hand, and styles of written preservation, on the other, has found a fresh boost amid the historiography of identity. Literacy itself is an old subject and its relationship with orality was outlined controversially by Walter Ong in 1982, some three years after Michael Clanchy's pathbreaking study of how and why the written record triumphed in medieval Britain.[21] Similarly the inevitability of oral history as a resource for African historians had become second nature: oral histories often supply their sole sources and function in tribal societies as an important, mobile history.[22] What has moved on in the literature is rather the use to which oral historical method is now put and the kind of subject currently attempted. In its early years of development in Britain, for example, Paul Thompson and others drew attention to the value of recollection to enrich areas of working-class history which the documentary record frequently failed to penetrate.[23] This subaltern flavour continues in a variety of areas of historical study in Britain and the US, especially when charged with the currents of postmodernism that push in the direction of examining racial minorities, the experience of women, the voice of the inarticulate mass.[24] War and social conflict exercise fascination still for their acting as nodes around which to weave

---

21 Michael Clanchy, *From Memory to Written Record: England 1066–1307* (1979); Walter J. Ong, *Orality and Literacy: The Technologizing of the Word* (1982).

22 E.g. Joseph C. Miller, *The African Past Speaks: Essays on Oral Tradition and History* (Folkestone, 1980); Jeffrey A. Fadiman, *An Oral History of Tribal Warfare: The Meru of Mt. Kenya* (Athens, Ohio, 1982); Jan Vansina, *Oral Tradition as History* (1985).

23 Note that he had begun his interest in oral history as a form as early as 1978: see Paul Thompson, *The Voice of the Past: Oral History* (Oxford, 1978).

24 Some recent titles include Gerard Hutchinson and Mark O'Neill, *The Springburn Experience: An Oral History of Work in a Railway Community from 1840 to the Present Day* (Edinburgh, 1989); Stuart Rintoul, *The Wailing: A National Black* [ie. Aborigine] *Oral History* (Port Melbourne, Victoria, 1993; Cornelia Heins, *The Wall Falls: An Oral History of the Reunification of the Germanies* (1994); Elizabeth Roberts, *Women and Families: An Oral History 1940–1970* (Oxford, 1995).

memories strongly retrieved from a period of intense awareness or suffering.[25]

In a sense, however, the potential of oral history within the new configurations of identity, memory, language and narrative is better reflected in the way in which it has begun to appear in areas *not* normally deemed natural to the method, such as international relations or diplomatic history.[26] Equally, the arrival of a series of publications devoted to this aspect of historical work such as Paul Thompson's *International Yearbook of Oral History and Life Stories*, complemented by the German periodical *Bios* on the European continent, emphasize both the centrality of the medium and the degree to which it has entwined itself in identity as its crucial problematic.[27] Of course, the interview method on which this approach rests confines its operation to the most recent periods; but it is not fanciful to see it operating as at least a category of aspiration in the study of medieval and early-modern popular culture where the relationship between the spoken and the written has lost its former simplicity and become a jungle to explore with an anthropological guidebook and an archaeological trowel.

Identity, memory, orality: each evolves its essence over time. None consists in a time-independent eruption or catastrophe but rather forms itself like a geological formation in which a world of 'before' and 'after' leaves its trace. To represent that sense of evolution-through-time (theorists use the description 'diachronic' when discussing it) historians traditionally construct a text dominated by narrative; and the revival of that practice in the last twenty years bears an important relation to the postmodern impetus considered in the previous section.

---

25 E.g. Neil MacMaster, *Spanish Fighters: An Oral History of Civil War and Exile* (Basingstoke, 1990); Ronald Fraser, *Blood of Spain: An Oral History of the Spanish Civil War* (1994); Wallace Terry (ed.), *Bloods: An Oral History of the Vietnam War of Black Veterans* (New York, 1984); Henry Hampton, *Voices of Freedom: An Oral History of the Civil Rights Movement from the 1950s through the 1980s* (New York, 1990).

26 Cf. Robert P. Gartwhol, Donita M. Moorhus and Douglas J. Wilson (eds), *Oral History and Postwar German–American Relations* (Washington, DC, 1997).

27 Volume 2 of the *Yearbook* (Oxford, 1993) was called *Between Generations: Family Models, Myths and Memories*; volume 3 was *Migration and Identity* (1994); volume 4 *Gender and Memory* (1996). Cf. *Bios: Zeitschrift für Biographieforschung und Oral History* (Leverkusen, 1988–).

On the other hand, the practice does not in itself imply commitment to postmodern persuasions in our own day any more than it did to Macaulay or Michelet. The most arch-realists, such as the late Sir Geoffrey Elton, can choose to employ narrative – thickened narrative, as Elton used to call it – in order to press the text as close as possible to the detailed transformations they are describing, without any sense that they are 'representing' the world in a mysterious form of fiction of the kind Barthes or Derrida would suppose. Thus, among new work appearing at the point of writing, a magisterial narrative of the Russian Revolution by Orlando Figes has a certain literary flamboyance. Its opening resembles romantic narrative in its lushness and willingness to go beyond documentary evidence for flavour and etched depiction:

> On a wet and windy morning in February 1913 St Petersburg celebrated three hundred years of Romanov rule over Russia . . . The city bustled with sightseers from the provinces, and the usual well-dressed promenaders around the Winter Palace now found themselves outnumbered by the unwashed masses – peasants and workers in their tunics and caps, rag-bundled women with kerchiefs on their heads. Nevsky Prospekt experienced the worst traffic jams in its history as trams and horse-drawn carriages, cars and sleighs, converged on it. The main streets were decked out in the imperial colours of white, blue and red; statues were dressed in garlands and ribbons; and portraits of the tsars . . . hung on the facades of banks and stores. Above the tram lines were strung chains of coloured lights, which lit up at night with the words 'God Save the Tsar' or a Romanov double-headed eagle and the dates 1613–1913. Out-of-towners, many of whom had never seen electric light, stared up and scratched their heads in wonderment. There were columns, arcs and obelisks of light . . . [28]

Yet this project has no more to do with postmodernism than with positivism: it proposes rather a return to a Carlylean vision of narrative as a means of evoking events in the imagination and supplying a sense of persuasive authenticity. Similarly, Ian Kershaw's vast biography of Hitler will make great use of narrative as a method of construction while rejecting the postmodern embrace with a certain Weberian contempt and Lancastrian violence.[29] When one turns, on yet another hand, to, say, John Demos's beautiful and arresting account of an

---

28 Orlando Figes, *A People's Tragedy: The Russian Revolution 1891–1924* (1996, 1997 edn), p. 3.
29 Ian Kershaw, *Hitler* (2 vols), forthcoming.

eighteenth-century identity crisis in a woman who was captured by native Americans and chose to stay captured rather than return to her former culture,[30] it becomes immediately apparent that the author's historical imagination is soaked in a postmodern concern with story, gender-inclusiveness and representation. It remains simply unclear at this point whether narrative structures and the resurgence of biography as a form betoken the effect of a Parisian saline drip or a sign that the patient has discharged himself to seek alternative medicine.

History has often followed where Thought – philosophy, psychology, sociology, anthropology – has led, though the historical community's cherished and admirable resistance to Thought has normally interpolated a time lag of several decades before the impact has become noticeable. That is why prediction becomes so pointless. It may become relevant all the same that the philosophers have already begun their back-lash against postmodern pessimism over the possibility of gaining historical truth and in thirty years' time we may see the historians back on its trail. One straw in the wind strikes the present writer and, since this has been a shamelessly personal account, there seems no harm in mentioning it. In the summer of 1998 the World Congress of Philosophy is hosting in Boston, among its other attractions, a panel on the philosophy of history. Of the three speakers, two will be philosophers and one an historian. The subject will be narrative and its relation to historical truth. Now just a couple of decades ago historians would have wagered good money on the philosophers' arguing against the possibility of historical truth and the historian's bleating that there was something in it. This occasion will see the reverse. Two professional philosophers will press the case for a 'realist' approach to historical knowledge and blow away the pretensions of postmodern confusion and cultural relativism. The historian, drawing less on epistemological theory than on a sense of what actually happens when history gets made by its practitioners, will find himself arguing the counter-case. Quaint, this. We seem to have reached an odd point in our evolution where it is the historian who has to preach the fragility of his own subject's truth-claims to those who have never tried to construct

---

30 John Demos, *The Unredeemed Captive: A Family Story from Early America* (New York, 1994).

them but none the less regard them as robust. Either the philosophers have not read enough historiography or the historian has read too much. At any rate the latter will almost certainly fail to convince a philosophical audience that relativism will not go away, that thoughtful historians suspect that their methods are inadequate to overcome doubts about attaining 'truth', and that historiography contains within its complexities and contestation the measure of our difficulty if not the solving of it.

I shall do my best.

REFERENCES

Adams, Henry Brooks (1889–90) *History of the United States during the Jefferson and Madison Administrations*, 9 vols, New York.
—— (1904) *Mont-Saint-Michel and Chartres*, London.
—— (1917) *The Education of Henry Adams*, Boston and New York.
Adams, Herbert Baxter (1882) *The Germanic Origins of New England Towns*, Baltimore.
Alison, A. (1833–42) *History of Europe during the French Revolution*, 10 vols, Edinburgh.
—— (1853–9) *History of Europe from the Fall of Napoleon in 1815 to the Accession of Louis Napoleon in 1852*, 8 vols, Edinburgh.
—— (1883) *Some Account of my Life and Writings: An Autobiography*, ed. Lady Alison, 2 vols, Edinburgh.
Allegra, L. and Torre, A. (1977) *La nascità dalla storia sociale in Francia dalla Commune alle Annales*, Turin.
Anderson, M. (1980) *Approaches to the History of the Western Family 1500–1914*, London.
—— (1987) *The 1851 Census: A Guide to the National Sample of the Enumerators' Returns*, Cambridge.
Andreski, S. (ed.) (1971) *Herbert Spencer*, London.
Andrews, W. L. (1985) *Critical Essays on W. E. B. Du Bois*, Boston.
Antoni, C. [1940] (1962) *From History to Sociology*, ed. H. White, New York.
Ashley, W. J. (1888–93) *An Introduction to English Economic History and Theory*, 2 vols, London.
Aydelotte, W. O. (1971) *Quantification in History*, Reading, Mass.
—— (ed.) (1977) *The History of Parliamentary Behavior*, Princeton.

—— et al. (eds) (1972) *The Dimensions of Quantitative Research in History*, London.

Bagehot, W. (1872) *The English Constitution*, 2nd edn, London.

Bailey, C. (1936) *Francis Fortescue Urquart: A Memoir*, London.

Baker, A. R. H. (1984) 'Reflections on the relation of historical geography and the *Annales* school of history', in A. R. H. Baker and D. Gregory (eds) *Explorations in Historical Geography*, Cambridge.

Bancroft, G. (1882) *History of the Formation of the Constitution of the United States of America*, 2 vols, New York.

Bann, S. (1984) *The Clothing of Clio: A Study of the Representation of History in Nineteenth-Century Britain and France*, Cambridge.

Barker, P. (1993) *Michel Foucault: Subversions of the Subject*, New York and London.

Barnes, H. E. [1937] (1962) *A History of Historical Writing*, New York.

Barraclough, G. (1978) *Main Trends in History*, New York.

Barthes, R. (1977) 'Introduction to the structural analysis of narrative', in R. Barthes, *Image, Music, Text*, London.

Bassett, J. S. (1917) *The Middle Group of American Historians*, New York.

Beard, C. and Beard, M. (1913) *An Economic Interpretation of the Constitution*, New York.

—— (1915) *The Economic Origins of Jeffersonian Democracy*, New York.

—— (1927) *The Rise of American Civilisation*, New York.

Beck, L. W. (ed.) (1963) *Kant on History*, Indianapolis.

Becker, C. L. (1901) *The Growth of Revolutionary Parties and Methods*, New York.

—— (1915) *The Beginnings of the American People*, New York.

—— (1932) *The Heavenly City of the Eighteenth-Century Philosophers*, New Haven, CT.

—— (1935a) *Detachment and the Writing of History*, New York.

—— (1935b) *Everyman his own Historian*, New York.

Bell, D. (1960) *The End of Ideology*, Glencoe, IL.

Ben-Israel, H. (1968) *English Historians on the French Revolution*, Cambridge.

Bentley, M. (1993) 'Victorian historians and the larger hope', in M. Bentley (ed.) *Public and Private Doctrine: Essays in British History Presented to Maurice Cowling*, Cambridge.

—— (ed.) (1997) *Companion to Historiography*, London.

Berg, M. (1996) *A Woman in History: Eileen Power 1889–1940*, Cambridge.

Berlin, I. (1976) *Vico and Herder*, London.

Bickel, C. (1991) *Ferdinand Tönnies: Soziologie als skeptische Aufklärung zwischen Historismus und Rationalismus*, Opladen.

Blaas, P. B. M. (1978) *Continuity and Anachronism: Parliamentary and Constitutional Development in Whig Historiography and in the Anti-Whig Reaction between 1890 and 1930*, The Hague.

Bloch, M. [1931] (1966) *French Rural Society: An Essay on its Basic Characteristics*, Berkeley and Los Angeles.

Bonfield, L., Smith, R. and Wrightson, K. (eds) (1986) *The World we have Gained: Histories of Population and Social Structure. Essays Presented to Peter Laslett on his Seventieth Birthday*, Oxford.

Bossuet, J. B. (1681) *Discours sur l'histoire universelle*, Paris.

Bossy, J. (1982) 'Some elementary forms of Durkheim', *Past and Present* 95: 3–18.

Boureau, A. (1990) *Histoires d'un historien: Kantorowicz*, Paris.

Breisach, E. (1983) *Historiography: Ancient, Medieval, and Modern*, Chicago.

Browning, O. (1910) *Memories of Sixty Years at Eton, Cambridge and Elsewhere*, London.

Buckle, H. T. [1857–61] (1894) *The History of Civilisation in England*, 3 vols, London. [2 vols, 1857–61.]

Burckhardt, J. [1860] (n.d.) *The Civilization of the Renaissance in Italy*, New York.

—— [1905] (1955) *Weltgeschichtliche Betrachtungen*, ed. J. Oeri, Stuttgart.

—— (1965) *Judgements on History and Historians*, New York.

Burger, T. (1976) *Max Weber's Theory of Concept Formation*, Durham, NC.

Burke, P. (1973) *A New Kind of History from the Writings of Lucien Febvre*, London.

—— (ed.) (1992) *New Perspectives on Historical Writing*, Philadelphia.

—— (1990) *The French Historical Revolution: The Annales School 1929–89*, Stanford.

Burrow, J. W. (1981) *A Liberal Descent: Victorian Historians and the English Past*, Cambridge.

—— (1985) *Gibbon*, Oxford.

Butterfield, H. [1931] (1973) *The Whig Interpretation of History*, Harmondsworth.

Cahnman, W. J. and Boskoff, A. (eds) (1964) *Sociology and History: Theory and Research*, New York.

Cairnes, J. E. (1875) *FR* 23/17 (Jan.).

Cam, H. M. (1944) *Liberties and Communities in Medieval England: Case Studies in Administration and Topology*, Cambridge.

—— (1962) *Law Finders and Law Makers in Medieval England*, London.

Campbell, I. (1993) *Thomas Carlyle*, Edinburgh.

Canary, R. H. and Kozick, H. (eds) (1978) *The Writing of History: Literary Form and Historical Understanding*, Madison.

Cannadine, D. (1993) *G. M. Trevelyan: A Life in History*, New York.

Caplan, J. (1989) 'Postmodernism, poststructuralism and deconstruction: notes for historians', *Central European History* 22: 260–78.

Carbonell, C.-O. (1976) *Histoire et historiens*, Toulouse.

—— and Livet, G. (eds) (1983) *Au Berceau des Annales*, Toulouse.

Carlyle, T. [1830] (1956) 'On history', in Stern 1956.

—— (1833–42) *The French Revolution*, 3 vols, London.

—— [1858–65] (1897) *History of Friedrich II of Prussia, called Frederick the Great*, 8 vols, London.

Carr, D. (1986) *Time, Narrative and History*, Bloomington.

Certeau, M. de (1988) *The Writing of History*, NY.

Chadwick, O. (1975) *The Secularization of the European Mind*, Cambridge.

Chartier, R. (1987) *The Cultural Uses of Print in Early-Modern France*, Princeton.

—— (1993) *Cultural History: Between Practices and Representations*, Cambridge.

—— (1994) *The Order of Books: Readers, Authors and Libraries in Europe between the Fourteenth and Eighteenth Centuries*, Cambridge.

Chickering, R. (1993) *Karl Lamprecht: A German Academic Life (1856–1915)*, Atlantic Highlands, NJ.

Chirot, D. (1984) 'The social and historical landscape of Marc Bloch', in T. Skocpol (ed.) *Vision and Method in Historical Sociology*, Cambridge.

Codazzi, A. (1985) *Hyppolyte Taine e il progetto filosofico di una storiografica scientifica*, Florence.

Coffa, J. A. (1991) *The Semantic Tradition from Kant to Carnap: To the Vienna Station*, ed. L. Wessels, Cambridge.

Cohen, G. A. (1979) *Karl Marx's Theory of History: A Defence*, Oxford.

Coleridge, S. T. [1830] (1976) *On the Constitution of the Church and State*, ed. J. Colmer, London.

Colley, L. (1989) *Lewis Namier*, London.

Collie, R. (1964) 'Johan Huizinga and the task of cultural history', *American Historical Review* 69: 607–30.

Collingwood, R. G. (1946) *The Idea of History*, ed. T. M. Knox, Oxford.

Comte, A. (1830–42) *Cours de philosophie positive*, 6 vols, Paris.

Condorcet, Marquis de (1795) *Esquisse d'un tableau des progrès de l'esprit humain*, Paris.

Conrad, A. H. and Meyer, J. R. (1958) 'The economics of slavery in the ante-bellum South', *Journal of Political Economy* 66: 95–130.

Conze, W. (1963) *Die deutsche Nation*, Göttingen.

—— (1964) *Die Zeit Wilhelm II und die Weimarer Republik*, Tübingen.

—— (1967) *Das deutsch–russische Verhältnis*, Göttingen.

Corbin, A. (1983) 'La *Revue historique*: analyse de contenu d'une publication rivale des *Annales*', in Carbonell and Livet 1983.

Coulanges, F. de (1864) *La Cité antique*, Paris.

Cowling, M. (1967) *1867: Disraeli, Gladstone and Revolution*, Cambridge.

Creighton, L. (1904) *Life and Letters of Mandell Creighton*, 2 vols, London.

Croce, B. (1941) 'History complete and incomplete', in B. Croce, *History as the Story of Liberty*, London.

Crossley, C. (1993) *French Historians and Romanticism: Thierry, Guizot, the Saint-Simonians, Quinet, Michelet*, London.

Culler, A. D. (1985) *The Victorian Mirror of History*, New Haven.

Cunningham, A. (1950) *William Cunningham, Teacher and Priest*, London.

Cunningham, W. (1882) *The Growth of English Industry and Commerce*, Cambridge.

—— (1896) *Modern Civilisation in some of its Economic Aspects*, London.

Darnton, R. (1984) *The Great Cat Massacre and Other Episodes in French Cultural History*, London.

—— (1995a) *The Corpus of Clandestine Literature in France 1769–89*, New York.

—— (1995b) *The Forbidden Bestsellers of Pre-Revolutionary France*, New York.

Dauphin, C., Farge, A., Fraisse, G. *et al.* (1986) 'Culture et pouvoir des femmes: essai d'historiographie', *Annales ESC* 41: 271–93.

Davies, R. R. (1967) 'Marc Bloch', *History* 52: 265–82.

Davis, N. Z. (1975) *Society and Culture in Early-Modern France: Eight Essays*, Stanford.

—— (1983) *The Return of Martin Guerre*, Cambridge, MA.

—— (1995) *Women on the Margins: Three Seventeenth-Century Lives*, Cambridge, MA.

Delbrück, H. (1924–8) *Weltgeschichte*, 5 vols, Berlin.

Dilthey, W. (1976) *Wilhelm Dilthey: Selected Writings*, ed. H. P. Rickman, Cambridge.

Dionisotto, C. (1989) *Ricordo di Arnaldo Momigliano*, Bologna.

Dosse, E. [1987] (1994) *New History in France: The Triumph of the Annales*, Chicago.

Dray, W. (1980) *Perspectives on History*, London.

Du Bois, W. E. B. (1903) *The Souls of Black Folk*, Chicago.

—— (1935) *Black Reconstruction*, New York.

Dunn, W. H. (1961–3) *James Anthony Froude: A Biography*, 2 vols, Oxford.

Eichhorn, K. F. (1821–3) *Deutsche Staats- und Rechtsgeschichte*, 3rd edn, Göttingen.

Elton, G. R. (1972) *Policy and Police*, Cambridge.

—— (1974–84) *Studies in Tudor and Stuart Politics*, 3 vols, Cambridge.

—— (1982) *The Tudor Constitution*, 2nd edn, Cambridge.

—— (1986) *The Parliament of England 1559–1581*, Cambridge.

—— (1991) *England under the Tudors*, 3rd edn, London.

Ermarth, M. (1978) *Wilhelm Dilthey: The Critique of Historical Reason*, Chicago.

Erwin, R. (1966) 'Civilization as a phase of world history', *American Historical Review* 71: 1181–98.

Evans, C. (1983) *The Making of the Micro: A History of the Computer*, Oxford.

Febvre, L. (1925) *Geographical Introduction to History*, New York.

—— (1942) *Le Problème de l'incroyance au XVIe siècle: la religion de Rabelais*, Paris.

—— (1953) *Combats pour l'histoire*, Paris.

Fentress, J. and Wickham, C. (1992) *Social Memory*, Oxford.

Fink, C. (1989) *Marc Bloch*, Cambridge.

Fletcher, A. (1995) *Gender, Sex and Subordination in England*, New Haven, CT.

Floud, R. (1979) *An Introduction to Quantitative Methods for Historians*, 2nd edn, London.

—— and McCloskey, D. (eds) (1994) *The Economic History of Britain since 1700*, 2nd edn, Cambridge.

Fogel, R. W. (1964) *Railroads and Economic Growth: Essays in Economic History*, Baltimore.

—— (1966) 'The new economic history: its findings and methods', *Economic History Review*, 25, 19: 642–56.

Fogel, R. W. and Elton, G. R. (1983) *Which Road to the Past? Two Views of History*, New Haven, CT.

Fogel, R. W. and Engerman, S. L. (1974) *Time on the Cross*, 2 vols, Boston and Toronto.

Forbes, D. (1952) *The Liberal Anglican Idea of History*, Cambridge.

Forster, J. (1839) *Oliver Cromwell 1599–1658*, 2 vols, London.

Forstman, J. (1977) *A Romantic Triangle: Schleiermacher and Early German Romanticism*, Missoula.

Foucault, M. (1966) *Les Mots et les choses*, Paris.

—— (1980) *Power/Knowledge: Selected Interviews and Other Writings 1972–77*, ed. C. Gordon, New York.

Frédéricq, P. (1899) *L'Enseignment supérieure de l'histoire*, Ghent.

Freeman, E. A. (1867–79) *The Norman Conquest of England*, 6 vols, Oxford.

Freund, J. (1992) *D'Auguste Comte à Max Weber*, Paris.

Froude, J. A. (1856–70) *The History of England from the Fall of Wolsey to the Defeat of the Spanish Armada*, 12 vols, London.

Fukuyama, F. (1992) *The End of History and the Last Man*, London.

Furet, F. (1984) *In the Workshop of History*, Chicago.

Galston, W. A. (1975) *Kant and the Problem of History*, Chicago.

Gardiner, P. (ed.) (1959) *Theories of History*, New York.

Gardiner, S. R. (1883–4) *History of England from the Accession of James I to the Outbreak of the Civil War*, 2 vols, London.

—— (1886–91) *History of the Great Civil War*, 3 vols, London.

—— (1894–1901) *History of the Commonwealth and Protectorate*, 3 vols, London.

—— (1909) *The Last Years of the Protectorate 1656–58*, London.

Gay, P. (1975) *Style in History*, New York.

Gerard, A. (1983) 'À l'origine du combat des *Annales*: positivisme historique et système universitaire', in Carbonell and Livet 1983.

Gibbon, E. [1776–88] (1909–14) *The History of the Decline and Fall of the Roman Empire*, ed. J. B. Bury, 7 vols, London.

Gilbert, F. (1990) *History: Politics or Culture?*, Princeton.

—— (ed.) (1975) *The Historical Essays of Otto Hintze*, Oxford.

Ginzburg, C. (1980) *The Cheese and the Worms: The Cosmos of a Sixteenth-Century Miller*, Baltimore.

—— (1983) *Night Battles: Witchcraft and Agrarian Cults in the Sixteenth and Seventeenth Centuries*, London.

—— (1990) *Myths, Emblems, Clues*, London.

—— (1991) *Ecstasies: Deciphering the Witches' Sabbath*, Harmondsworth.

Goldstein, L. J. (1976) *Historical Knowing*, Austin.

Gombrich, E. (1970) *Aby Warburg: An Intellectual Biography*, London.

Gooch, G. P. (1913) *History and Historians in the Nineteenth Century*, London.

Gossman, L. (1990) *Between History and Literature*, Cambridge, MA.

Gray, J. (1995) *Isaiah Berlin*, London.

Grumley, J. E. (1989) *History and Totality: Radical Historicism from Hegel to Foucault*, London.

Guizot, F. (1829–32) *Histoire de la civilisation en France*, 5 vols, Paris.

Haddock, B. (1980) *An Introduction to Historical Thought*, London.

Hae-song, H. (1992) *Booker T. Washington and W. E. B. Du Bois: A Study in Race Leadership. 1895–1915*, Seoul.

Hartog, F. (1988) *Le XIXe siècle et l'histoire: le cas Fustel de Coulanges*, Paris.

Haskins, C. H. (1923) *The Rise of Universities*, New York.

—— (1927) *The Renaissance of the Twelfth Century*, Cambridge, Mass.

Hawthorne, G. (1991) *Plausible Worlds: Possibility and Understanding in History and the Social Sciences*, Cambridge.

Hay, D. (1977) *Annalists and Historians: Western Historiography from the Eighth to the Eighteenth Centuries*, London.

Hettling, M. et al. (1991) *Was ist Gesellschaftsgeschichte? Positionen, Themen, Analysen*, Munich.

Higham, J., Krieger, L. and Gilbert, F. (1965) *History*, Englewood Cliffs.

Hintze, O. (1915) *Hohenzollern und ihr Werk*, 5th edn, Berlin.

Hodges, R. and Whitehouse, D. (1983) *Charlemagne and the Origins of Europe: Archaeology and the Pirenne Thesis*, London.

Hofstadter, R. (1968) *The Progressive Historians*, New York.

Hoggart, R. (1957) *The Uses of Literacy*, London.

Holly, M. A. (1984) *Panofsky and the Foundation of Art History*, Ithaca, NY.

Howe, M. A. de Wolfe (1908) *The Life and Letters of George Bancroft*, 2 vols, London.

Hufton, O. (1995) *The Prospect before her: A History of Women in Western Europe*, 1: *1500–1800*, London.

Hughes, H. S. (1959) *Consciousness and Society: The Reorientation of European Social Thought 1890–1930*, New York.

Huizinga, J. [1919] (1924) *The Waning of the Middle Ages*, London. (Tr. of: *Herfstij der Middeleeuven*, 1919.)

Hull, R. (1992) *In Praise of Wimps: A Social History of Computer Programming*, Hebden Bridge.

Hume, D. (1754–62) *History of England from the Invasion of Julius Caesar to the Revolution of 1689*, 6 vols, London.

Hunt, L. (ed.) (1989) *The New Cultural History*, Berkeley.

Iggers, G. G. (1983) *The German Conception of History: The National Tradition of Historical Thought from Herder to the Present Day*, Middletown, CT.

Jacobitti, E. E. (1981) *Revolutionary Humanism and Historicism in Modern Italy*, New Haven, CT.

Jameson, F. (1981) *The Political Unconscious: Narrative as a Socially Symbolic Act*, London.
—— (1991) *Postmodernism, or, the Cultural Logic of Late Capitalism*, London.
Jann, R. (1985) *The Art and Science of Victorian History*, Columbus, OH.
Kaegi, W. (1962) *Europäische Horizonte im Denken Jacob Burckhardts. Drei Studien*, Basle and Stuttgart.
Kantorowicz, E. H. (1957) *The King's Two Bodies: A Study in Medieval Political Theology*, Princeton.
Kemble, J. M. (1849) *The Saxons in England*, London.
Kenyon, J. (1983) *The History Men: The Historical Profession in England since the Renaissance*, London.
Kern, S. (1983) *The Culture of Time and Space 1880–1920*, London.
Keylor, W. R. (1975) *Academy and Community: The Foundation of the French Historical Profession*, Cambridge, Mass.
Knies, C. (1883) *Die politischen Oekonomie vom Standpunkte der geschichtlichen Methode*, 2nd edn, Brunswick.
Koselleck, R. (1985) *Futures Past: On the Semantics of Historical Time*, Cambridge, MA.
——, Lutz, H. and Rüsen, J. (eds) (1982) *Formen der Geschichtsschreibung*, Munich.
Kozicki, H. (ed.) (1993) *Western and Russian Historiography: Recent Views*, Basingstoke.
Krieger, L. (1977) *Ranke: The Meaning of History*, Chicago.
Krohn, C.-D. (1993) *Intellectuals in Exile: Refugee Scholars and the New School for Social Research*, Amherst.
Krüger, D. (1983) *Nationalökonomie in wilhelminischen Deutschland*, Göttingen.
Kuczynski, J. (1978) *Porträt eines Gesellschaftswissenschaftlers*, Berlin.
LaCapra, D. (1983) *Rethinking Intellectual History: Texts, Contexts, Language*, Ithaca, NY.
—— (1985) *History and Criticism*, Ithaca, NY.
Lamprecht, K. (1885–6) *Deutsches Wirtschaftsleben im Mittelalter*, 3 vols, Leipzig.
—— (1896) *Alte und neue Richtungen in der Geschichtswissenschaft*, 2 vols, Berlin.
—— (1900) *Die kulturhistorische Methode*, Berlin.
—— (1914) *Krieg und Kultur: Drei vaterländische Vorträge*, Leipzig.
Langlois, C. V. and Seignobos, C. (1898) *Introduction to the Study of History*, London.
Laslett, P. [1965] (1971) *The World we have Lost*, 2nd edn, London.
—— (1996) *A Fresh Map of Life: The Emergence of the Third Age*, Basingstoke.
Lawler, E. G. (1986) *David Friedrich Strauss and his Critics: The* Life of Jesus *Debate in Early Nineteenth-Century German Journals*, New York.
Le Quesne, A. C. (1982) *Carlyle*, Oxford.
Lefebvre, G. (1924) *Les Paysans du Nord pendant la Révolution française*, 2 vols, Paris and Lille.

—— (1932) *La Grande Peur de 1789*, Paris.

—— (1934) *Foules historiques*, Paris.

—— (1937) *Les Thermidoriens*, Paris.

Lefranc, A. (1925) *Le Visage de François Rabelais*, Melun.

—— (1932) *L'Œuvre de Rabelais d'après les recherches les plus récentes*, Groningen.

Lehmann, H. and Melton, J. Van Horn (eds) (1994) *Paths of Continuity: Central European Historiography from the 1930s to the 1950s*, Cambridge.

Lehmann, H. and Sheehan, J. L. (eds) (1991) *An Interrupted Past: German-Speaking Refugee Historians in the United States after 1933*, Cambridge.

Le Roy Ladurie, E. [1978] (1982) *Montaillou: Cathars and Catholics in a French Village 1294–1324*, London.

—— (1984) *Love, Death and Money in the Pays d'Oc*, Harmondsworth.

Letwin, S. R. (1965) *The Pursuit of Certainty*, Cambridge.

Levi, G. (1988) *Inheriting Power: The Story of an Exorcist*, Chicago.

Levison, W. (1946) *England and the Continent in the Eighth Century*, Oxford.

Liebel, H. P. (1963/4) 'Philosophical Idealism in the *Historische Zeitschrift* 1859–1914', *History and Theory* 3: 316–30.

Lilla, M. (1993) *G. B. Vico: The Making of an Anti-modern*, Cambridge, MA.

Linehan, P. (1992) *Past and Present in Medieval Spain*, Aldershot.

Lixl-Purcell, A. (1988) *Women in Exile: German-Jewish Autobiographies since 1933*, New York.

Loewenberg, B. J. (1972) *American History in American Thought*, New York.

Lowenthal, D. (1985) *The Past is a Foreign Country*, Cambridge.

Luden, H. (1825–37) *Geschichte des deutschen Volkes*, 12 vols, Gotha.

Lukes, S. (1973) *Emile Durkheim: His Life and Work*, London.

Lukoff, H. (1979) *From Dits to Bits: A Personal History of the Electronic Computer*, Portland, OR.

Lutz, R. (1990) 'Lamprecht-Streit und französischer Methodenstreit: der Jahrhundertwende in vergleichender Perspektive', *Historische Zeitschrift* 251: 325–63.

Lyon, B. (1974) *Henri Pirenne*, Ghent.

Lyotard, J. (1984) *The Postmodern Condition*, Manchester.

Macaulay, T. B. [1828] (1956) 'History', in Stern 1956.

—— (1849–61) *History of England*, 5 vols, London.

McClelland, C. E. (1971) *German Historians and England: A Study in Nineteenth-Century Views*, Cambridge.

McClelland, P. D. (1975) *Causal Explanation and Model Building in History, Economics and the New Economic History*, Ithaca, NY.

McNeill, W. H. (ed.) (1967) *Essays in the Liberal Interpretation of History by Lord Acton: Selected Papers*, Chicago.

—— (1989) *Arnold J. Toynbee: A Life*, New York.

Maine, H. J. S. (1861) *Ancient Law*, London.

Maitland, F. (1936) *Selected Essays*, Cambridge.

—— [1901] (1957) 'William Stubbs, Bishop of Oxford', in H. Cam (ed.) *F. W. Maitland: Historical Essays*, Cambridge.

Maner, J. R. (1982) 'Theory and practice of history in the French and German Enlightenment', unpublished Ph D. thesis, Chapel Hill, NC.

Marías, J. (1990) *Understanding Spain*, Ann Arbor.

Martin, G. H. and Spufford, P. (1990) *The Records of the Nation: The Public Record Office 1838–1988*, Woodbridge.

Mathiez, A. (1922–7) *La Révolution française*, 3 vols, Paris.

—— (1929) *La Réaction thermidorienne*, Paris.

—— (1934) *Le Directoire*, Paris.

Mauss, M. (1925) *Essai sur le don*, Paris.

Megill, A. (1985) *Prophets of Extremity: Nietzsche, Heidegger, Foucault, Derrida*, Berkeley.

Meinecke, F. (1924) *Die Idee der Staatsräson in der neueren Geschichte*, Berlin.

—— (1936) *Entstehung des Historismus*, Munich and Berlin.

—— (1946) *Die deutsche Katastrophe*, Wiesbaden.

—— (1972) [1936] *Historism: The Rise of a New Historical Outlook*, London.

Menger, K. (1994) *Reminiscences of the Vienna Circle and the Mathematical Colloquium*, ed. L. Golland, B. McGuiness and A. Sklar, Dordrecht.

Meyer, J. (1993) *Bossuet*, Paris.

Michelet, J. (1833) *Principes de la philosophie de l'histoire, traduits de la Scienza Nuova de J. B. Vico par Jules Michelet*, Brussels.

Millgate, J. (1973) *Macaulay*, London.

Mink, L. O. (1969) *Mind, History and Dialectic*, Indianapolis.

Momigliano, A. (1955–92) *Contributi alla storia degli classici (e del mondo antico)*, 9 vols, Rome.

—— (1966) *Studies in Historiography*, London.

—— (1977) *Essays in Ancient and Modern Historiography*, Oxford.

Mommsen, W. J. and Osterhammel, J. (eds) (1987) *Max Weber and his Contemporaries*, London.

Monod, G. (1895) *Du Rôle de l'opposition des races et des nationalités dans la dissolution de l'empire carolingien*, Paris.

—— (1896) *Études critiques sur les sources de l'histoire carolingienne*, Paris.

Montesquieu, C.-L. de (1749) *De l'esprit des lois*, Geneva.

Moore, J. (1981) *W. E. B. Du Bois*, Boston.

Munz, P. (1977) *The Shapes of Time: A New Look at the Philosophy of History*, Middletown, CT.

Muratori, L. A. *Antiquitates italicae medii aevi*, Milan.

Namier, J. (1971) *Lewis Namier: A Biography*, London.

Niethammer, L. (1992) *Posthistoire: Has History Come to an End?*, London.

Novick, P. (1988) *That Noble Dream: The 'Objectivity Question' and the American Historical Profession*, Cambridge.

Oakeshott, M. (1932) *Experience and its Modes*, Cambridge.

—— (1983) *On History*, Oxford.

O'Gorman, F. (1989) *Voters, Patrons and Parties: The Unreformed Electoral System of Hanoverian England 1734–1832*, Oxford.

Onians, J. (ed.) (1994) *Sight and Insight: Essays on Art and Culture in Honour of E. H. Gombrich at 85*, London.

Owensby, J. (1994) *Dilthey and the Narrative of History*, Ithaca, NY.

Palmer, B. (1989) *Descent into Discourse: The Reification of Language and the Writing of Social History*, Philadelphia.

Panofsky, E. (1970) *Meaning in the Visual Arts*, Harmondsworth.

Peardon, T. P. (1933) *The Transition in English Historical Writing, 1760–1830*, New York.

Peel, J. D. Y. (1971) *Herbert Spencer*, London.

Phillips, J. A. (1982) *Electoral Behavior in Unreformed England: Plumpers, Splitters and Straights*, Princeton.

Pidal, R. M. (1929) *La España del Cid*, 2 vols, Madrid.

—— (1940–54) *Historia de España*, 4 vols, Madrid.

Pirenne, H. (1910) *Les Anciennes Démocraties des Pays Bas*, Paris.

Pirenne, J. (1945–56) *Les Grands Courantes de l'histoire universelle*, 7 vols, Neuchâtel.

Plantinga, T. (1980) *Historical Understanding in the Thought of Wilhelm Dilthey*, Toronto.

Popper, K. (1957) *The Poverty of Historicism*, London.

Porter, R. (1988) *Edward Gibbon: Making History*, London.

Postan, M. (1971) *Fact and Relevance*, Cambridge.

Randa, A. (1954) *Handbuch der Weltgeschichte*, 2 vols, Olten and Freiburg im Breisgau.

Ranke, L. von (1824) *Geschichte der romanischen und germanischen Völker von 1494 bis 1535*, Berlin.

—— (1840) *The Ecclesiastical and Political History of the Popes of Rome during the Sixteenth and Seventeenth Centuries*, 3 vols, tr. S. Austin, London. (First published as: *Die römischen Päpste, ihre Kirche und ihr Staat im 16. und 17. Jahrhundert*, 3 vols, Berlin, 1834–6.)

—— (1852–6) *Französische Geschichte vornehmlich im sechszehnten und siebzehnten Jahrhundert*, Stuttgart and Tübingen.

—— (1859–69) *Englische Geschichte vornehmlich im siebzehnten Jahrhundert*, Berlin.

—— (1973) *The Theory and Practice of History*, ed. G. G. Iggers and K. von Moltke, Indianapolis.

Rebérioux, M. (1983) 'Le Débat de 1903: historiens et sociologues', in Carbonell and Livet 1983.

Reill, P. H. (1975) *The German Enlightenment and the Rise of Historicism*, Berkeley.

Reynolds, S. (1994) *Fiefs and Vassals: The Medieval Evidence Re-interpreted*, Oxford.

Richardson, R. (ed.) (1991) *Schleiermacher in Context: Papers from the 1988 International Symposium on Schleiermacher at Herrnhut*, Lewiston, NY and Lampeter.

Rickert, H. [1896] (1986) *The Limits of Concept Formation in Natural Science: A Logical Introduction to the Historical Sciences*, ed. G. Oakes, Cambridge.

Rickman, H. P. (1979) *Wilhelm Dilthey: Pioneer of the Human Studies*, London.

Ricœur, P. (1984) *The Reality of the Historical Past*, Milwaukee.

—— (1984–8) *Time and Narrative*, 3 vols, Chicago.

Rigby, S. H. (1987) *Marxism and History: A Critical Introduction*, Manchester.

Roberts, J. (1976) *The Hutchinson History of the World*, London.

Robertson, W. (1759) *History of Scotland*, 2 vols, London.

—— (1777) *History of America*, 2 vols, London.

Robinson, J. H. (1912) *The New History*, New York.

—— (1921) *The Mind in the Making*, New York.

—— (1937) *The Human Comedy*, New York.

—— and Beard, C. A. (1907–8) *The Development of Modern Europe*, 2 vols, New York.

Robinson, R., Gallagher, J. and Denny, A. (1961) *Africa and the Victorians*, London.

Rose, N. (1980) *Lewis Namier and Zionism*, Oxford.

Rosenberg, J. D. (1985) *Carlyle and the Burden of History*, Oxford.

Rostovtzeff, M. (1926) *Social and Economic History of the Roman Empire*, Oxford.

—— (1926–7) *A History of the Ancient World*, 2 vols, Oxford.

—— (1941) *The Social and Economic History of the Hellenistic World*, 3 vols, Oxford.

Rotenstreich, N. (1987) *Time and Meaning in History*, Dordrecht and Boston.

Roth, M. (1995) *The Ironist's Cage: Memory, Trauma and the Construction of History*, New York.

Rothfels, H. (1920) *Carl von Clausewitz*, Berlin.

—— (1924) *Bismarcks englische Bündnispolitik*, Stuttgart.

—— (1934) *Bismarck und der Osten*, Leipzig.

—— (1935) *Ostraum, Preussentum und Reichsgedanke*, Leipzig.

—— (1949) *Die deutsche Opposition gegen Hitler*, Krefeld.

Rüsen, J. (1983–6) *Grundzüge einer Historik*, 2 vols, Göttingen.

Schmoller, G. (1898) *Umrisse und Untersuchungen zur Verfassungs-, Verwaltungs- und Wirtschaftsgeschichte besonders des preussischen Staates im 17. und 18. Jahrhundert*, Leipzig.

Schön, M. (1987) 'Gustav Schmoller and Max Weber', in Mommsen and Osterhammel 1987.

Scott, J. (1992) 'Women's history', in Burke 1992.

Seeley, J. (1883) *The Expansion of England*, London.

—— (1895) *The Growth of British Policy*, 2 vols, Cambridge.

Semmel, B. (1984) *John Stuart Mill and the Pursuit of Virtue*, New Haven.

Sheehan, J. J. (1978) *German Liberalism in the Nineteenth Century*, Chicago.

—— (1989) *German History 1770–1866*, Oxford.

Sidgwick, A. and Sidgwick, E. M. (eds) (1906) *Henry Sidgwick: A Memoir*, London.

Siegel, M (1983) 'Henry Berr et la *Revue de synthèse historique*', in Carbonell and Livet 1983.

Simiand, F. (1932) *Le Salaire. L'évolution sociale et la monnaie*, 3 vols, Paris.

Simon, C. (1988) *Staat und Geschichtswissenschaft in Deutschland und Frankreich 1871–1914*, 2 vols, Berne.

Simon, W. M. (1968) 'Power and responsibility: Otto Hintze's place in German historiography', in L. Krieger and F. Stern (eds) *The Responsibility of Power: Historical Essays in Honor of Hajo Holborn*, London and Melbourne.

Skinner, Q. (ed.) (1985) *The Return of Grand Theory in the Human Sciences*, Cambridge.

Slee, P. R. H. (1986) *Learning and a Liberal Education: The Study of Modern History in the Universities of Oxford, Cambridge and Manchester 1800–1914*, Manchester.

Smith, C. W. (1956) *Carl Becker: on History and the Climate of Opinion*, Ithaca, NY.

Smith, R. J. (1987) *The Gothic Bequest*, Cambridge.

Sorensen, D. (1983) *Carlyle's Method of History in 'The French Revolution'*, Edinburgh.

Sparvel-Bayly, E. (ed.) (1902) *Life and Letters of H. Taine*, 3 vols, n.p.

Spencer, H. (1855) *Social Statics*, London.

—— (1904) *Autobiography*, 2 vols, London.

Spengler, O. [1918–23] (1926–9) *The Decline of the West*, 2 vols, London.

Standley, A. (1981) *Auguste Comte*, Boston.

Steinberg, M. P. (1988) *The Presence of the Historian: Essays in Honour of Arnaldo Momigliano*, Middletown, CT.

Stenton, F. M. (1932) *The First Century of English Feudalism 1066–1166*, Oxford.

—— (1943) *Anglo-Saxon England*, Oxford.

Stern, F. (ed.) (1956) *Varieties of History: From Voltaire to the Present*, New York.

Stieg, M. F. (1986) *The Origin and Development of Scholarly Historical Periodicals*, Alabama.

Stoianovich, T. (1976) *French Historical Method: The 'Annales' Paradigm*, Ithaca, NY.

Sweet, P. R. (1978–80) *Wilhelm von Humboldt: A Biography*, 2 vols, Columbus, OH.

Taine, H. (1874–93) *Les Origines de la France contemporaine*, 6 vols, Paris.

Taylor, A. J. P. (1961) *The Origins of the Second World War*, London.

Taylor, M. (1992) *Men versus the State*, Oxford.

Tenbruck, F. H. (1987) 'Max Weber and Eduard Meyer', in Mommsen and Osterhammel 1987.

Thorpe, B. (1840) *Ancient Laws and Institutes of England*, 2 vols, London.

Tilly, C. (1972) 'Quantification in history, as seen from France', in V. R. Lorwin and J. N. Price (eds) *The Dimensions of the Past: Materials, Problems and Opportunities for Quantitative Work in History*, New Haven.

Tönnies, F. (1926) *Gemeinschaft und Gesellschaft*, 7th edn, Berlin.

—— (1931) *Einführung in die Soziologie*, Stuttgart.

Toynbee, A. (1934–61) *A Study of History*, 12 vols, London.

Treitschke, H. von (1879–94) *Deutsche Geschichte im neunzehnten Jahrhundert*, 5 vols, Leipzig.

Trevor-Roper, H. (1984) 'Jacob Burckhardt', *Proceedings of the British Academy* 70: 359–78.

Tucker, M. (ed.) (1991) *Literary Exile in the Twentieth Century: An Analysis and Biographical Dictionary*, New York.

Turner, F. J. (1921) *The Frontier in American History*, New York.

—— (1932) *The Significance of Sections in American History*, New York.

Turner, S. (1799–1805) *History of England from the Earliest Period to the Norman Conquest*, London.

Valdes, M. (1991) *A Ricœur Reader: Reflection and Imagination*, London.

Venturi, F. (1952) *Il populismo russo*, 2 vols, Turin.

—— (1971) *Utopia and Reform in the Enlightenment*, Cambridge.

—— (1972) *Italy and the Enlightenment*, London.

—— (1977) *Les Intellectuels, le peuple*, 2 vols, Paris.

—— (1980) *Venezia nel secondo settecento*, Turin.

—— (1988) *Giovinezza di Diderot (1713–53)*, Palermo.

Vickery, A. (1993) 'Golden Age to separate spheres? A review of the categories and chronology of English women's history', *Historical Journal* 36: 383–414.

Vico, G. B. (1708) *De nostri temporis studiorum ratione*, Naples.

—— (1710) *De antiquissima Italorum sapientia ex linguae latinae originibus eruenda*, 3 vols, Naples.

—— (1982) *Selected Writings*, ed. L. Pompa, Cambridge.

Vinogradoff, P. (1892) *Villainage in England*, Oxford.

—— (1905) *The Growth of the Manor*, London.

Voegelin, E. (1975) *From Enlightenment to Revolution*, Durham, NC.

Volpe, G. (1907) *Eretici e moti ereticali sociale dal XI al XIV secolo*, 2 vols, Milan.

—— (1928) *Guerra, dopoguerra, fascismo*, Venice.

—— (1939) 'Storia del movimento fascista', in B. Mussolini (ed.) *La dottrina del fascismo*, Rome.

—— (1943–52) *L'Italia moderna*, Florence.

Waitz, G. (1844–78) *Deutsche Verfassungsgeschichte*, 8 vols, Kiel.

—— (1864) *Deutsche Kaiser von Karl dem Grossen bis Maximilian*, 5 vols, Berlin.

Walsh, W. H. (1976) 'The logical status of Vico's ideal eternal history', in G. Tagliacozzo and D. Verene (eds) *Giambattista Vico's Science of Humanity*, Baltimore.

—— [1951] (1992) *An Introduction to the Philosophy of History*, Bristol.

Waugh, E. (1962) *Ronald Knox: A Biography*, London.

Weber, M. (1958) *The Protestant Ethic and the Spirit of Capitalism*, New York.

Weinberg, J. (1988) *Where Three Civilizations Meet: A Tribute to the Life and Work of Arnaldo Dante Momigliano*, London.

Wes, M. A. (1990) *Michael Rostovtzeff, Historian in Exile*, Stuttgart.

White, H. (1973) *Metahistory: The Historical Imagination in Nineteenth-Century Europe*, Baltimore.

—— (1980) *Tropics of Discourse: Essays in Cultural Criticism*, Baltimore.

—— (1987) *The Content of the Form: Narrative Discourse and Historical Representation*, Baltimore.

Whitrow, C. J. (1988) *Time in History: Views of Time from Prehistory to the Present Day*, Oxford.

Wiener, M. (1981) *English Culture and the Decline of the Industrial Spirit*, Harmondsworth.

Wiggerhaus, R. (1994) *The Frankfurt School: Its History, Theories and Significance*, Cambridge.

Wilcox, D. F. (1987) *The Measure of Times Past: Pre-Newtonian Chronologies and the Rhetoric of Relative Time*, Chicago.

Williams, R. (1958) *Culture and Society*, London.

Windelband, W. (1894) *Geschichte und Naturwissenschaft*, Strasbourg.

Winkel, H. (1977) *Die deutsche Nationalökonomie im 19. Jahrhundert*, Darmstadt.

Winter, E. J. (1961) *August Ludwig v. Schlözer und Russland*, Berlin.

Wolin, R. (1992) *The Terms of Cultural Criticism: The Frankfurt School, Existentialism, Poststructuralism*, New York.

Wrigley, E. A. (1987) *People, Cities and Wealth: The Transformation of Traditional Society*, Oxford.

—— (1988) *Continuity, Chance and Change: The Character of the Industrial Revolution in England*, Cambridge.

—— and Schofield, R. S. (1989) *The Population History of England 1541–1871*, Cambridge.

Wücher, A. (1956) *Theodor Mommsen. Geschichtsschreibung und Politik*, Göttingen.

Yovel, Y. (1980) *Kant and the Philosophy of History*, Princeton.

FURTHER READING IN ENGLISH

The references in the main text will best help those who want to follow a particular theme in more detail. Broader histories of historical writing will be found in Michael Bentley (ed.), *Companion to Historiography* (London, 1997), B. A. Haddock, *An Introduction to Historical Thought* (1980) and Ernst Breisach, *Historiography: Ancient, Medieval and Modern* (Chicago, 1994). Arnaldo Momigliano, *The Classical Foundations of Modern Historiography* (Berkeley, 1990) introduces readers without Italian to some of his best essays. For the European theme generally, see Georg G. Iggers, *New Directions in European Historiography* (rev. edn, 1985). For the American, start with Peter Novick, *That Noble Dream: The 'Objectivity Question' and the American Historical Profession* (Cambridge, 1988). Postmodernism has received a variety of treatments of which Keith Jenkins, *Rethinking History* (1991) is the most simple and polemical. For a European perspective, see Jerzy Topolski (ed.), *Historiography between Modernism and Postmodernism* (Amsterdam, 1994). Earlier periods than those treated here are analysed with sophistication in Simon Hornblower, *Greek Historiography* (Oxford, 1996) and Gabrielle M. Spiegel, *The Past as Text: The Theory and Practice of Medieval Historiography* (Baltimore, 1997).

Important theoretical approaches to historiography as a form have appeared in recent years. These are reflected in an overview of *A New Philosophy of History*, edited by Frank Ankersmit and Hans Gellner (1995). Two French studies are especially significant: Paul Veyne, *Writing History: An Essay on Epistemology* (Ann Arbor, 1997) and Michel de Certeau, *The Writing of History* (New York, 1988). In America, Hayden White's difficult but often remarkable essays are collected in *The Content of Form: Narrative Discourse and Historical Representation* (Baltimore, 1987). For recent reactions against this style of thought, see the works referred to in my 'Postscript'.

Serious students looking for more detailed guidance could begin with Susan K. Kinnell, *Historiography: An Annotated Bibliography of Journal Articles, Books and Dissertations* (Santa Barbara, Calif., 1987).

INDEX

(Names of people merely mentioned in the text are not included and I have also excluded most contemporary historians except for those discussed at some length. For a fuller index, see the *Companion to Historiography*, pp.974–97.)